YOU'VE

YOU'VE GOT MAIL

The Messages to the Seven Churches of Asia (Revelation 2–3)

Stephen Travis

First published in 1995 by The Bible Reading Fellowship
This edition published in 2002 by Spring Harvest Publishing Division
and Authentic Lifestyle
Reprinted 2002

08 07 06 05 04 03 02 8 7 6 5 4 3 2

Authentic Lifestyle is an imprint of
Authentic Media, PO Box 300, Kingstown Broadway,
Carlisle, Cumbria CA3 0QS, UK
and Box 1047, Waynesboro, GA 30830-2047, USA
www.paternoster-publishing.com

British Library Cataloguing-in-Publication Data
A catalogue record for this book is available from the British Library

ISBN 1–85078–449–3

Cover design by Diane Bainbridge
Printed in Great Britain by
Cox & Wyman Ltd, Reading, Berkshire

Contents

Preface

The aim of this book is to help today's readers sit alongside the first readers of the book of Revelation and hear afresh what the living Christ has to say to his people. It would be easy, perhaps, to use the tough messages to the seven churches as a peg on which to hang my own frustrations and complaints about today's church. I have tried not to do that. For the message of these chapters is a searching message, but it is a hopeful one. As we listen to his verdict on the life of first-century churches we see aspects of our own church life mirrored in theirs. And we hear his challenge and his promise of renewal.

Most of the chapters include some practical suggestions for responding to the message of the letters to the churches. Though mostly brief, these are not intended to offer cut-and-dried answers, but rather to stimulate thought and reaction by the reader. At the end of each chapter are questions for personal reflection or group discussion, designed to help people apply the message to their local situation.

Although the fall of the communist regimes of Eastern Europe in 1989 mostly brought to an end the persecution of Christians by those states, intolerance and hostility remain the daily experience of Christians in many countries today. Reading from the book of Revelation makes us aware of the pressures which they face and draws us closer to them. It reminds us how much we have to learn from the words of Christ to those who before us have followed him in a hostile world.

This book would never have existed without the work of Dr Colin Hemer, who was Research Fellow at Tyndale House in Cambridge until his early death in 1987. He had written an outstanding scholarly study of *The Letters to the Seven Churches of Asia in their Local Setting* (JSOT Press, Sheffield, 1986), which he planned to make available to a wider public in a more popular form. The book which he was left no time to undertake, I have attempted to write. I have leaned heavily on his research, and gladly pay tribute to this meticulous scholar and Christian gentleman.

Stephen Travis

*I*John, your brother and companion in the suffering and kingdom and patient endurance that are ours in Jesus, was on the island of Patmos because of the word of God and the testimony of Jesus. On the Lord's Day I was in the Spirit, and I heard behind me a loud voice like a trumpet, which said: "Write on a scroll what you see and send it to the seven churches: to Ephesus, Smyrna, Pergamum, Thyatira, Sardis, Philadelphia and Laodicea."

I turned round to see the voice that was speaking to me. And when I turned I saw seven golden lampstands, and among the lampstands was someone "like a son of man", dressed in a robe reaching down to his feet and with a golden sash round his chest. His head and hair were white like wool, as white as snow, and his eyes were like blazing fire. His feet were like bronze glowing in a furnace, and his voice was like the sound of rushing waters. In his right hand he held seven stars, and out of his mouth came a sharp double-edged sword. His face was like the sun shining in all its brilliance.

When I saw him, I fell at his feet as though dead. Then he placed his right hand on me and said: "Do not be afraid. I am the First and the Last. I am the Living One; I was dead, and behold I am alive for ever and ever! And I hold the keys of death and Hades.

"Write, therefore, what you have seen, what is now and what will take place later. The mystery of the seven stars that you saw in my right hand and of the seven golden lampstands is this: The seven stars are the angels of the seven churches, and the seven lampstands are the seven churches.

Revelation 1:9–20

CHAPTER 1

The reigning Christ and the church under pressure

(Revelation 1)

I met Jonathan at a party. As he filled his plate with black-currant cheesecake we introduced ourselves.

'Haven't I heard your name somewhere before?', he mused. And he dragged from the back of his mind the memory that he had once read one of my books. 'But I'm not in this Christian thing any more', he continued, with a directness which surprised me.

'Perhaps what you read put you off', I ventured, defensively.

'Oh no', he replied, 'it wasn't anything you wrote. I just couldn't cope with the church any more.'

And he disappeared with his cheesecake into the mêlée of guests, leaving me to ponder on his words. Were they a feeble excuse? A justified criticism? Or perhaps one of those comments out of the blue which makes you think again about something you would rather not face up to?

The church is under fire from many directions. People like Jonathan criticize it for being restrictive rather than liberating, for protecting the institution rather than responding imaginatively to human needs and hopes.

Young people, if they consider it at all, wonder why the average local church seems so far away from their own lives and concerns.

I too get angry with the church – the energy it spends on maintaining its own life rather than bringing Christ's light to the world, the pettiness and lack of vision which characterizes so much of its internal argument. I am haunted by some words of D.H. Lawrence:

> *I know the greatness of Christianity: it is a past greatness. I know that, but for those early Christians, we should never have emerged from the chaos and hopeless disaster of the Dark Ages. If I had lived in the year 400, pray God, I should have been a true and passionate Christian. The adventurer.... But now I live in 1924, and the Christian venture is done. The adventure is gone out of Christianity. We must start on a new venture towards God.*

Then I get angry with myself for thinking so negatively about my Christian brothers and sisters. I am troubled by the thought: If all Christians were like me, would God's work flourish or fail? And I see that there is another question which matters more than whether Jonathan or I or anyone else is angry with the church: How does Christ himself view the church? Maybe we have to face up to the tough questions he wants to ask if we are to find a way through to being the church he intends us to be.

As it happens, the last book of the Bible introduces us to seven churches which faced the searching gaze of the risen

Christ. They came under fire from his truth, his demanding love. If we listen with them we may hear his words of warning and renewal, and find a new direction for our Christian communities.

Churches ancient and modern

But think for a moment about the church with which you are associated. How long have Christians been worshipping there? What resources does it have, in people, in buildings, in the financial support of its members? What networks of friendship and influence has it built up in the neighbouring community? What links does it have with other churches? You may smile at these questions, thinking more of the problems in your church than of its advantages and opportunities. But compare it with the churches which first received John's Revelation.

If you live in the centre of Belfast, for example, you can find over two hundred churches within ten miles of your home. But these churches of the first century are separated from each other by thirty or forty miles of countryside. Outside the cities most people have not yet heard of Christianity. The churches are mostly quite small communities in cities of some size. They have no long-standing Christian tradition, no New Testament, no church buildings. They are scattered and fragile. Their circumstances are not promising.

They are 'the seven churches in the province of Asia' (1:4). This province of the Roman empire stretched two hundred

miles eastwards from the western coast of what we now call
Turkey. The seven churches were not the only Christian
groups in the province. Colossae, for example, to which Paul
wrote a letter, was in Asia. But the seven perhaps had particular links with John, the writer of Revelation.

Tradition assumes that the author of the book was John
the apostle. But he does not identify himself as an apostle,
and we must be content simply to know that he was a ser-
vant of Christ (1:1), entrusted with an urgent message for
his people.

Companions in suffering

'I, John, your brother and companion in the suffering and
kingdom and patient endurance that are ours in Jesus, was
on the island of Patmos because of the word of God and the
testimony of Jesus' (1:9). While he was on Patmos John
received the visions which he recorded in the book of
Revelation. The island lies forty miles off the south-west-
ern coast of Turkey, and today is a tranquil place, untroubled
by the throb of all-night discos which disturbs the air of
many another Greek island.

But it was hardly tranquil for John, since he had been
banished there because of his Christian witness. We do not
know the circumstances of his deportation. But probably
someone in Asia, resenting his fearless witness, had brought
accusations against him to the provincial governor. The
governor in turn decided that exile to Patmos would be a
convenient way of avoiding any repetition of the problem.

So John shares with his group of churches the experience of suffering for Christ's sake, and he has every reason to believe that this suffering is going to intensify. The time is about AD 95. The last three decades have been filled with events which made it seem as if the world was coming off its hinges – earthquakes, military coups in Rome, the Jewish Revolt of AD 66 which led in AD 70 to the destruction by the Romans of Jerusalem and its temple. This last devastating event was to Christians a fulfilment of Jesus' predictions and a pointer towards his final coming.

In AD 81 Domitian became emperor. He suffered from an inferiority complex, and his insecurity increasingly made him suspect that enemies in Rome were keen to do away with him. To bolster his position he began to demand that his subjects should worship him as 'lord and god'. To worshippers of another Lord this was an ominous development.

Pressure from Jews and Gentiles

It is often imagined that during the reign of Domitian and other emperors of this period there was widespread persecution and martyrdom of Christians. In fact, there is little concrete evidence for such an idea. But Domitian's rule was becoming increasingly totalitarian, and the safety of Christians could certainly not be taken for granted. In Asia itself the Christians found themselves squeezed between two opposing dangers.

There was pressure from Jews. There were many Jews in Asia, and many converts to Christianity there were either

Jews, or Gentiles who had been attracted to Judaism and
had attached themselves to the synagogue (see Acts 2:9;
13:16, 26, 43; 14:1; 19:8). Judaism was a 'recognized religion' which Jews were allowed to practise wherever they
lived, and the Roman authorities did not at first distinguish
Christians from Jews.

But after the catastrophe of AD 70, the situation changed.
The emperor decreed that the annual tax paid by all adult
Jewish men towards the upkeep of the Jerusalem temple
should now be diverted to Jupiter's temple in Rome.
Payment of the tax was a sign that Jews accepted Rome's
authority over them.

How did this affect Christians? After AD 70 animosity
between Jews and Christians increased, because Christians
generally saw the destruction of Jerusalem as divine judgment on the Jewish people. The separation between church
and synagogue gathered pace. This left Christians in a very
exposed position. As long as they – or at least the Jewish
believers among them – could maintain their Jewishness,
they could claim the protection which was offered under
the law to Jews. But now it was open to any Jew who
resented the growth of the Christian movement to inform
the authorities that the local Christians were not Jews at all.
If Christians tried to remain under the cover of Judaism by
offering to pay the tax to Jupiter, Jews could protest that
they were not genuine Jews. If they did not pay the tax, that
only proved they were not Jews and laid them open to suspicion of being a dangerous new cult.

Disowned by Jews, the followers of Jesus could find no
protection from pagan society either. People in the

provinces of the empire demonstrated their loyalty to Rome by taking part in worship of Rome and of the emperor. Such worship did not of course involve religious devotion as we would understand it. The performance of certain rituals at the temple was simply a way of expressing political submission to the power of Rome and its emperor. There were temples specially dedicated to this purpose in Smyrna, Pergamum, Ephesus and other Asian cities. Probably the ordinary citizen did not actively participate in the cult – that could be left to the civic dignitaries who took a lead in such matters. But once a Christian had been exposed as a potential trouble-maker, he would be expected to demonstrate his loyalty by offering worship to Rome and its emperor.

We know for certain that this is what happened a few years later in Bithynia (in northern Turkey). About AD 112 the provincial governor Pliny wrote to the emperor Trajan about Christians who had been brought to his attention. If people insisted on remaining Christians, he wrote, he ordered them to be executed. But if they said they never had been Christians, or had given up Christianity, he let them go, provided they offered incense to a statue of the emperor, prayed to the gods of Rome and cursed Christ. Trajan replied that Pliny was doing exactly the right thing.

So the Christians of Asia certainly had the feeling of being under fire. They were under threat from the Jews from whom they had once derived some protection. They faced the possibility of an uncomfortable ride with the pagan authorities. The temptation to keep a low profile and avoid mention of Christ in any conversation must have been very great. If only they kept quiet, they might be left undisturbed.

The power of the gods

Apart from the possibility of falling foul of the governing authorities in this way, there was the constant pressure of the pagan atmosphere which surrounded every Christian. As they walked the streets they were always conscious of the temples and statues of pagan gods, the obscene graffiti which covered many a wall, and the symbols of the old fertility cults which retained a prominent place in popular religion. If we today are exposed to the potentially harmful influence of the media, the absence of television and advertising hoardings in first-century Asia did not leave people free from such onslaughts on their minds.

The gods themselves were not simply remote mythical figures. They represented powerful forces which hold sway over human lives. For example, Aphrodite (called Venus by the Romans) represented the sexual urge which affects us all, enriching or ruining our lives. Dionysus was the god of wine, representing the power of alcohol both to inspire hospitality and the arts, and to provoke the destructive madness of the 'lager-lout' and the 'soccer hooligan'. Hermes (or Mercury) was not simply the mythical messenger of the gods, propelled by the wings on his sandals, but represented the world of trade and finance. And when people worshipped these gods in their temples they were acknowledging the power of these forces and trying to ensure that their influence was beneficial rather than destructive.

Although Christians had given up worshipping these gods, they knew the continuing power of all that they represented. We too may dismiss as childish the stories which were told about the gods, but we are just as likely as any ancient Greek to be seduced by the ruinous power of sex, or alcohol, or money or a thousand other 'idols'.

The church and the reigning Christ

That is the world in which the churches of Asia lived. In recording the Lord's words to the seven churches in Revelation 2 and 3, John presents us with a vision of how Christ wants the church to be. This is the kind of church we need to be, if we are to respond to the challenge that confronts us, whether the date is AD 95 or 2005.

John, who knows these churches intimately, understands what they face. More importantly, Christ himself understands. Through his death and resurrection he is 'the faithful witness, the firstborn from the dead, and the ruler of the kings of the earth' (1:5). In calling them to bear their witness faithfully in the face of everything that threatens them, he is asking them to follow closely in his own footsteps. He is 'ruler of the kings of the earth' not because he batters his opponents into submission by force. For him, and therefore for his followers, victory comes through suffering. That is the strange, distinctive message of the Christian gospel.

To reassure his readers as they face an uncertain future, John records a vision of the risen Christ (1:12–18). This picture, drawn partly from Old Testament descriptions of God, expresses the awesome majesty of Christ in a way which fits the situation of the Christians of Asia. As we shall see, most of the seven letters which follow refer back to one aspect or another of this vision of Christ. For the moment we notice two things.

First, in verse 13 Christ is the 'one like a son of man' who in Daniel 7:13–14 received from God a kingdom that would never be destroyed. But he also has the hair 'white as wool' which in Daniel 7:9 belonged to God himself. By such use of imagery John declares that Jesus is one God with the Father. He is also 'the First and the Last' (1:17) – God's own title in Isaiah 44:6.

Second, through his resurrection Jesus holds power over death. 'I am the Living One; I was dead, and behold I am alive for ever and ever! And I hold the keys of death and the world of the dead' (verse 18, my translation). So his followers can give themselves to his service, whatever the risks, in the confidence that their ultimate future is secure in him.

Lampstands, stars and angels

The Christ whom John sees in his vision is walking among seven golden lampstands and holds seven stars in his right hand (verses 12–13, 16). The lampstands represent the seven churches (verse 20). Christ, whose divine glory is normally hidden from his people, is nevertheless always present with them. He does not sympathize with their suffering and danger from a safe distance, but is especially close to the church which bears the scars of its obedience to him.

Christ holds the seven stars in his hand. These stars are explained as representing 'the angels of the seven churches' (verse 20). In the Greek and Roman world it was widely believed that the movement of the seven planets controlled people's lives and destinies. Roman emperors took the symbol of the seven stars, depicting them on their coins, as if to say in their arrogance, '*We* rule the world, and don't you forget it!' But now Christ himself – who set the planets in their courses and is 'ruler of the kings of the earth' – reminds us that he is the true sovereign of the world.

But who are 'the angels of the seven churches', and why are the stars identified with them? In Jewish thought there was the idea that each nation has an angel who is a heavenly representative or symbol of the earthly nation, perhaps rather as Uncle Sam and John Bull are symbols of the American and British nations (see Dan. 10:13, 20-21; 12:1). So these angels are heavenly counterparts of the seven churches. These communities are very earthly, even earthbound. Yet at the same time they are 'in Jesus' (verse 9). There is a dimension to their lives which is true of no other earthly community. As lampstands, they bear the Light of the world. As stars, they are gripped by Christ's protecting hand. And we can see how easily John moves between thinking of the earthly churches and thinking of the angels as their heavenly counterpart when we notice that in 1:4, 11 he writes to the seven churches, but at the beginning of the letter to each individual church the instruction is, 'To the angel of the church in ... write'.

The writer of the book of Revelation is John, but its real author is the risen Christ. John is the prophet through whom he speaks, just as God addressed Israel through the Old Testament prophets. The message to each church begins, 'These are the words of...', which sounds like the familiar 'Thus says the Lord' of the prophets of Israel. We should perhaps speak not of the 'letters', but of the 'prophetic messages' to the seven churches. But in this book we shall continue to use the more familiar term 'letters'.

If the seven churches are under fire from their pagan and Jewish environment, they are also under fire from Christ. 'I hold this against you...', or words to that effect, is a repeated theme in the letters. If the church is to renew its life, it must face the penetrating gaze of its Lord.

Christ knows each church and holds it in his care

The messages to the seven churches reveal an intimate knowledge of the churches and the cities in which they are set. We shall see this from the remarkable way in which they allude to aspects of the life of each church and city. John the writer knows his churches well. But, more importantly, the risen Christ who is the real sender of these messages knows the churches, their strengths and weaknesses, the pressures they face, the faithfulness of their discipleship.

But his knowledge of the churches is not the knowledge of a headmaster checking up on his pupils' misdeeds or of a detective uncovering crimes in unexpected places. It is more like the knowledge of parents who know the temptations to which their children are prone and yet stand by them through thick and thin. The Christ whose glory is portrayed in the vision of Revelation 1 holds the churches in his hand. However weak they are, he protects them. However much they fail in their responsibilities, he wants them to know that he holds them in his care.

When we are despairing or angry about the level of vitality in our churches and in ourselves, we can take encouragement from that. For all our faults, he hasn't given up on us.

The seven letters each follow a fairly standard pattern, which is set out here so that there is no need to labour the point as we go through the letters one by one:

- Address to the angel of the church (each local church has an angel who 'represents' it before God)

- Description of Christ, the author, in terms appropriate to the particular church

- Description of the church's deeds, followed by praise or criticism

- Warning of the consequences of unfaithfulness

- Exhortation to stand firm, and a promise to those who 'overcome' through their faithfulness

Real churches – then and now

The seven churches are real churches in real places, and the messages to the individual churches are arranged in the order which would be naturally followed by a messenger from Patmos arriving by sea at Ephesus. But John's intention is not to speak to each church in isolation from the other six. For each letter ends with the significant phrase, 'Let anyone who has an ear listen to what the Spirit is saying to the *churches*'. Each letter addresses the specific situation of the church addressed, but it contains a message which the other churches are meant to overhear and learn from.

In Revelation the number seven symbolizes completeness. So the churches of Asia are not simply isolated groups of Christians. There is a sense in which each one stands for, and is part of, the whole church of the first century and of all time. The letters meant for them are meant for us also.

But let's be honest. Not all churches today are looking for an urgent message from their living Lord. We listen to preachers and hope they have something interesting to say. But they had better not go on too long, and if they make us feel uncomfortable we'll accuse them of 'getting at us' and dismiss their comments as 'another of their hobby-horses'. In that way we can keep our links with the church without it disturbing us too much. But what if Christ really wants to speak to us through the experience of those churches of Asia and through the messages which he spoke to them? What if, out of love for a struggling or puzzled or complacent church, he wants to shake us to the foundations and point us in new directions? Have we ears to 'hear what the Spirit is saying to the churches'?

Most churches today have little sense of belonging to a worldwide community, enriched by varied histories and varied cultures. We have little sense of fellowship with Christians in other places from whom we might learn, or Christians facing particular trials and needing our love and support. Even within one nation, the suburban church is often blissfully ignorant of the life of the urban congregation five miles away. The urban congregation may have little knowledge even of the group of Asian Christians who hire its own premises for their meetings. Both may imagine (wrongly) that ministry in a rural parish is a bed of roses.

The letters to the seven churches can remind us all that an individual church, isolated from others, is not in God's scheme of things. Each church needs to listen for what God may want to say to it. But each church must also listen to what it can learn from God's message to others. For the particular danger which may have befallen one church is a potential danger for any church. And members of a family cannot afford to ignore the experience of their brothers and sisters.

Questions for reflection and discussion

1. What particularly in this chapter has helped you or made you think?

2. Have you met people like Jonathan (page 1)? What would you want to say to him about his difficulty in coping with the church as he has experienced it?

3. Think about the words of D.H. Lawrence (page 2). Is it a fair criticism of the church? What do you think an 'adventurous church' would look like?

4. Think about the description of Christ in Revelation 1:5. How would it help the readers to live with hostility from their neighbours and the possibility of persecution from the state?

5. What relationship does your church have with others? What benefits do such relationships bring? How might a stronger link with a particular church, in your own country or overseas, help to create a greater sense of belonging with each other and learning from each other?

*T*o the angel of the church in Ephesus write:
These are the words of him who holds the seven stars in his right hand and walks among the seven golden lampstands: I know your deeds, your hard work and your perseverance. I know that you cannot tolerate wicked men, that you have tested those who claim to be apostles but are not, and have found them false. You have persevered and have endured hardships for my name, and have not grown weary.

Yet I hold this against you: You have forsaken your first love. Remember the height from which you have fallen! Repent and do the things you did at first. If you do not repent, I will come to you and remove your lampstand from its place. But you have this in your favour: You hate the practices of the Nicolaitans, which I also hate.

He who has an ear, let him hear what the Spirit says to the churches. To him who overcomes, I will give the right to eat from the tree of life, which is in the paradise of God.

Revelation 2:1-7

CHAPTER 2

The Church at Ephesus – faithful but unloving

(Revelation 2:1-7)

Ephesus was the natural first stop for a messenger reaching mainland Turkey from Patmos. Let's imagine what John's messenger would see as he disembarked at the harbour, so that we can begin to appreciate what it felt like to be a Christian in this great city. As we shall see soon, what to us might look like the attractive description of a travel brochure, would be to him a catalogue of pressures on the church.

The messenger's eye would first be led eastwards along a broad street, flanked by gymnasiums and other sports facilities, to the magnificent 25,000-seat theatre, and upwards to Mount Pion rising behind it. The road north from the theatre would take him to the temple of Artemis. Artemis – called Diana by the Romans – was the mother-goddess who guaranteed the fertility of the earth. Her temple was one of the seven wonders of the ancient world. It was the largest building in the Greek world, and the first such structure to be built entirely of marble. Thirty-six of its 127 pillars were sculptured and overlaid with gold.

Devotion to Artemis was passionate, not only because the blessing of the mother-goddess seemed essential for the healthy continuation of life, but also because she helped to ensure the commercial prosperity of the city. The selling of religious objects such as silver statues of the goddess was big business, as Paul had found out to his discomfort (Acts 19:23-41). At the very time when John's *Revelation* was being written, the emperor Domitian boosted the temple's influence by extending the precinct which surrounded it.

Worship of the emperor

South of the theatre the messenger would see the commercial centre where the silversmiths had their workshops, and beyond it the temple dedicated to the worship of Domitian. Inside was a statue of the emperor himself, four times life size. Its head depicted the emperor as Zeus, the ruler of all the gods. There could be no more vivid reminder of his totalitarian demands.

This is the city where John's messenger arrived. With a population of 250,000, it was the fourth largest city in the world, after Antioch, Alexandria and Rome itself. Its strategic importance derived from its position on the western coast of Asia. Main trade routes from the east reached the sea at this point, and it was the ideal port for the voyage between Asia and Rome. The Greek geographer Strabo called it the market place of Asia Minor. Its inhabitants lived much closer together than people in cities of Europe and North America today, and because of the climate they spent much more time in the open air than we do. This made privacy difficult – you couldn't sneeze without half the neighbourhood knowing. But it also made opportunities for conversation, including the sharing of the Christian message, frequent.

The church to which John writes is set in this huge and prosperous city, conscious of its political and religious prestige. The church too is proud of its history. But it cannot take its position for granted. For wherever Christians live and work in this city, they cannot escape the influences that surround them. As Paul had found in his encounter with the silversmiths, the power of business and commerce to harass Christians is enormous if it finds that its own interests are being undermined by the gospel. The temple of Artemis, with its grounds recently extended, signifies an old religion renewing its strength – just as in the late twentieth century, the pre-Christian religions of Britain and North America hold new fascination for many people influenced by the New Age movement. And Domitian's recently built temple reminds people constantly of his totalitarian power.

The church's Lord

At the beginning of each letter Christ draws attention to some aspect of his character already described in the vision of chapter 1. Before the church can receive words of criticism or warning, it needs to hear about the Lord who loves it and protects it. He 'holds the seven stars in his right hand and walks among the seven golden lampstands' (verse 1).

Christ holds the stars – the seven churches – like a string of jewels. The image would not be lost on John's readers. When Domitian's young son died in 83, he proclaimed him to be a god, and coins were minted which showed his mother Domitia as queen of heaven and the child sitting on a globe, playing with the stars. Against such bizarre pretensions, Christ is proclaimed as the Lord of the universe who holds each church in his care. The churches may be weak, imperfect, a disappointment to their Lord. But still he blesses them with his presence.

'I know...' (verse 2). To each church the same phrase is used. Of course he knows. At first it sounds threatening, this idea that Christ knows all about my church and about all the things I would rather keep hidden. But on second thoughts, it's a relief to realize that he knows. He understands better than we do ourselves our situation, our successes and failures, our hopes and fears. When we stop pretending otherwise, we are ready to make progress. For the One who knows all about us is the One who can change us.

Jesus commends the Christians at Ephesus for three things (verses 2–3).

He praises their hard work. They know that the church is no place for spiritual picnicking, it is not a club for the religiously inclined. It is a place for demanding and constant obedience to Christ.

He praises their perseverance in the face of suffering and opposition. In this respect they outshine the modern church, where qualities such as perseverance and loyalty are in short supply. In an age of instant coffee, instant glue and

instant bank loans, we don't take easily to the pain of stick-
ing to unglamorous tasks, or developing a discipline in
prayer. But, as Samuel Chadwick said, 'All God's things are
grown things. He is never in the ready-made business.'

They have refused to tolerate false teachers. And this
has not just been a thoughtless gut reaction to new ideas:
'You have tested those who claim to be apostles but are not,
and have found them false'. The Lord's approval of their
resistance to a distorted Christianity could hardly be put
more strongly than it is in verse 6. What you hate, he says, I
also hate.

A distorted gospel

What was the nature of this false teaching? The false apostles (verse 2) were probably not simply charlatans aiming to
deceive the church, but people who at some time had
received authority to teach and had now become unbalanced in their message. In an attempt to come to terms with
the society in which they lived, they had succumbed to the
spirit of the age.

The false teachers are 'Nicolaitans' (verse 6) – followers
of someone called Nicolaus, though we have no inde-
pendent information about him. They are advocates of
'Christian freedom'. We can imagine them quoting with
enthusiasm some of Paul's slogans: 'It is for freedom that
Christ has set us free.' 'Where the Spirit of the Lord is,
there is freedom.' 'It is by grace you have been saved,
through faith – and this not from yourselves, it is the gift

of God – not by works, so that no-one can boast' (Gal. 5:1;
2 Cor. 3:17; Eph. 2:8). Christ has delivered us, they would
say, from everything that held us in bondage – our fear of
Fate and our powerlessness to control our own lives, our
anxiety about death and the future, the oppressive
demands of severe moral codes such as the Jewish Law.
Such a message would be attractive in Ephesus. It would
appeal to the anxieties of ordinary people, without
demanding any radical change in lifestyle. Salvation is for
the soul, and how you behave with your body will make
no difference to it.

That is how heresies nearly always develop. People take
one side of the truth – a real truth but without other truths
to balance it – and they push it to the limit. The Nicolaitans
have learnt well that Christ has liberated us from slavish
obedience to religious regulations. But they have ignored
the complementary truth: 'You, my brothers, were called to
be free. But do not use your freedom to indulge your sinful
nature' (Gal. 5:13).

In the early 1970s a friend of mine visited a community recently set up by a vibrant Christian group
calling themselves the Children of God. He came away
overwhelmed by their spiritual vitality, their openness and
deep commitment to each other. They had captured
something central to real Christianity. But in the following years they became what they are today – a sect
denying some basic Christian doctrines, dominated by
unbalanced leadership. And the original expression of
broth-erly love has been transformed into the offer of 'free
love' as an enticement to join the sect.

Testing new teachings

Like the church at Ephesus, we are expected to *test* whether new teachings are in harmony with the message passed on to us from the apostles. This does not mean throwing out every new idea as dangerous or demonic. But it does mean asking questions such as: Is this teaching consistent with what we know of Jesus and his attitude? Does it conflict with a central truth, such as the divinity of Christ or the reality of his resurrection? Is it in tune with the overall thrust of biblical teaching or does it take one small aspect of that teaching and exaggerate it to the exclusion of other aspects?

For instance, it would be tragic if Christians played down the importance of respecting our God-given natural environment simply because 'green' issues are an important aspect of New Age teaching. But it is equally tragic when Christians, seduced by New Age's green and attractive image, come under the spell of this movement. For it over-emphasizes human experience and personal fulfilment at the expense of self-giving. It looks for spirituality in the occult and in the religion of our pre-Christian ancestors. It resists the idea that any one religion may express the Truth. Its grasp of some important issues is a challenge to us. But its smile is the smile of a crocodile saying grace before lunch.

Another heresy today is the so-called 'Prosperity Gospel', which promises that Jesus will make you healthier and wealthier, and implies that suffering and weakness indicate a failure to claim God's promises. The message wins supporters because it is what people would like to believe and because it can appeal to the promises – particularly in Deuteronomy – that Israel's obedience will be blessed by God. But can you imagine it being endorsed by Jesus, who pronounced a blessing on the poor and said it was easier for a camel to squeeze through the eye of a needle than for a rich man to get into the kingdom of God? And what about John, who could promise his friends in Asia that they would reach the presence of God only through suffering and even martyrdom?

The totalitarian power of a ruler requires another kind of testing by Christians. How far is it right to obey him? At what point does resistance become the proper Christian response? When a regime is delivering stability and prosperity to its subjects, the temptation is to accept the benefits and keep quiet about the abuse of power or the oppression of minorities. In the nineteen-thirties and forties the 'German Christians', as they called themselves, chose to close their eyes to Nazi atrocities rather than disturb national unity and put their own security at risk.

For Christians today, the temptation is to accept for ourselves the tax cuts and the promises of increased prosperity offered by governments, rather than ask the painful questions about whether the government's policy which may benefit us is harming the vulnerable groups in society. Even in the most democratic society, a government wants to keep power and therefore appeals to the self-interest of the voters who, it thinks, can produce the majority it needs. But as Christians we are called to see a wider picture, to ask how a government is affecting not just ourselves, but the nation and the world.

A church without love

The church of Ephesus has spotted the danger in the teaching of the Nicolaitans. Unwearyingly they have refused to give space to such menacing novelties. But they too have failed to hold in balance two sides of their faith. In their zeal for truth they have forgotten love. 'I hold this against you; you have forsaken your first love. Remember the height from which you have fallen! Repent and do the things you did at first' (verses 4–5). It is a devastating message. On hearing it, the church's first reaction might well be to protest: 'But we are showing our love for God by defending his truth against all these attempts to undermine the true gospel.' But the word of the risen Christ cannot be denied.

Imagine a situation today. A church, established in 1907 after a notable mission to the town by a famous evangelist, stands in a now unfashionable district. Its congregation, drawn from a wide area, are people who appreciate the biblical teaching which they receive Sunday by Sunday. The minister does his homework well, and from time to time relates the teaching of scripture carefully to some controversial issue on which they look to him for guidance. Last month it was abortion and genetic research. At Easter he showed in detail why they should reject modern interpretations of the resurrection which do not accept that Jesus rose physically, leaving the tomb empty. Three years ago they successfully campaigned against the opening of a sex shop near the town centre.

This church is buoyant, with a strong sense of its mission and its identity as a place where the true gospel is preached.

Yet there is a hardness about it. Strangers who venture
inside are mostly ignored, or are questioned about their
credentials rather than welcomed warmly. When invited by
St James' Church, which they regard as 'liberal', to share in
a march of witness on Good Friday, the church council
voted against it for fear of compromising the gospel. Across
the road from the church in a run-down building is an
advice centre serving the multi-ethnic community of the
district. It suffers constantly from lack of resources and
people to help.

A passion for truth is a dangerous thing unless it is
wedded to Christ-like love. The Ephesians have set out to
contend for the truth, only to discover that in the course of
the battle they have lost the one quality without which all
others are worthless. Where love for other people is lost,
love for God turns into religious formalism, or fanaticism.

The recovery of love

How is love to be recovered? How is the balance to be
maintained between a passion for truth and a commitment
to love? The Christians at Ephesus need to reflect on what
they have already heard from the apostle Paul a generation
earlier, and our imaginary downtown church would be wise
to eavesdrop on their reflections.

● It is right to be on the lookout for teachings that distort the gospel of Christ, as Paul warned the elders of
   the church at Ephesus in his final tearful meeting with

them: 'I know that after I leave, savage wolves will
come in among you and will not spare the flock. Even
from your own number men will arise and distort the
truth in order to draw away disciples after them. So be
on your guard!' (Acts 20:29-31). And in the letter he
wrote to them earlier Paul had warned of the danger
of such teaching: 'Let no one deceive you with empty
words'. By this he meant the words of those who, in
the name of religion, advocated immoral behaviour
(Eph. 5:5-6). And he knew that Christians are engaged
in a spiritual battle with evil forces which seek to
blunt the effectiveness of the church's witness (Eph.
6:10-20).

● Yet there is a danger that opposition to false teaching
will turn into hatred for the false teachers. They are
labelled as heretics and cease to be treated as people for
whom God cares. But talk to people who have turned
from being Jehovah's Witnesses into being Christians
with an orthodox and living faith, and most of them
will tell you that the change came about because someone loved and listened to them and cared about them as
people.

● Another danger is that Christians who differ from ourselves on comparatively minor points of teaching or
practice come to be regarded as misguided, or at least as
rivals to our own superior brand of Christianity. The
Letter to the Ephesians has perspectives on this which
must be heard. Listen to what it says about love.

● All of us are utterly dependent on the love of Christ for
us (Eph. 1:4–6; 2:4). Without that we are lost. Because of
it we all have a special place in God's purpose.

● Because our security depends on Christ's love rather than
on our own insights or achievements we are expected to
love all God's people (Eph. 1:15). We are not entitled to
be more exclusive than God himself is.

● God's love among his people is a love which breaks down
barriers between people who might otherwise be suspi-
cious and dismissive of each other. Whether we like it or
not, we cannot belong to the people of God without
belonging to each other (Eph. 2:11–21).

● Love is not simply something which we have to strain to
produce within ourselves. It is a quality which we receive
from God and which flows through us as we ask him to
change us into more Christ-like people (Eph. 3:16–19).

● The fact that God is one, the Father of a single family,
means that we are to 'make every effort to keep the unity
of the Spirit through the bond of peace' (Eph. 4:3–6).

● A mark of Christian maturity is the ability not to be
taken in or thrown off course by clever teaching which
distorts true Christianity. But the ability to recognize
truth and reject falsehood can never be gained at the
expense of love, because growing deeper into Christ is
always a growing deeper into love. We are to 'speak the

truth in love', or to 'maintain the truth in a spirit of love'. There is no Christian truth which is not 'rooted and established in love' (Eph. 4:14–16; 3:17).

● To practise love is to reflect the character and concerns of God as he has shown himself to us in Jesus.

● This love is a matter not of mere talk or emotion but of action in down-to-earth ways. It affects such practical issues as our attitude to sex, the kind of jokes we make, what we do with our money, and whether we live in a spirit of thankfulness (Eph. 5:2–20).

● The letter's final greeting underlines the link between God's love for us and our love for him and for each other: 'Peace to the brothers, and love with faith from God the Father and the Lord Jesus Christ. Grace to all who love our Lord Jesus Christ with an undying love' (Eph. 6:23-24). So if we ask how love is to be recovered, we may answer: By drawing close to Jesus, and rediscovering his heartbeat. D.L. Moody recorded his own experience:

> *I took the word 'love' and I do not know how many weeks I spent in studying the passages in the Bible in which it occurs, till at last I could not help loving people. It just flowed out of my fingers. I got to thinking of the compassion of Christ. So I took out the Bible and began to read it over to find out what it said on the subject. At last the thought of his infinite compassion overpowered me. I could only like on the floor of my study, with my face in the open Bible, and cry like a child.*

A warning and a promise

A recovery of love is no optional extra. The situation is so serious that the Ephesians may cease to exist as a local church. 'If you do not repent, I will come to you and remove your lampstand from its place' (verse 5). It is possible for a local church so completely to cease living in a Christian way, that it ceases to be a church of Christ. It has become an empty shell, where his presence is unrecognizable.

But love can rise again. And those who 'overcome' (verse 7) are promised eternal life. With this reference to victory, John has especially in mind those who may suffer a martyr's death because of their faith. Like the death of their Lord, their death will mean triumph, not defeat. But the promise of eternal life embraces all who are faithful to Christ, whether or not their faithfulness leads to martyrdom.

The image by which John describes the promise of eternal life is carefully chosen. 'The tree of life, which is in the paradise of God' (verse 7) recalls the description of the Garden of Eden in Genesis 2:9. According to Jewish tradition, the original perfection of Eden would be restored in the paradise of the future, and the tree of life would feed God's people for ever.

But also people in Ephesus would recall that the temple of Artemis stood on what was originally a shrine associated with a sacred tree, and coins of Ephesus frequently portray a tree as an emblem of Artemis. And the temple was surrounded by its own sacred space or 'garden'. So the promise to those who are victorious is a message issued in defiant contrast to the seduction of Artemis and her cult. In Christ there is real security, real hope, in contrast to the attractive claims of seemingly all-powerful contemporary cults and movements.

'Let anyone who has an ear listen to what the Spirit is saying to the churches' (verse 7). With these words, repeated at the end of every letter, Christ makes clear that the message is for all the churches. It is easy for readers of a passage such as this to make a mental note of other churches and other Christians to whom it applies, and ask no questions about the quality of their own love. But if Ephesus, perhaps the greatest church of its day, must take care lest it should fall, how much more the rest?

Questions for reflection and discussion

1. What particularly in this chapter has helped you or made you think?

2. 'I know your deeds, your hard work and perseverance' (Rev. 2:2). Do you agree that perseverance is in short supply in today's 'instant society'? How can we encourage it in the church?

3. Look at the description of the Nicolaitans and of some modern distortions of Christian truth (pages 23, 24). Do you see evidence of any of these in Christian groups which you know? How can we commend a fuller understanding of the Christian message to people attracted to these 'alternatives'?

4. Imagine that you have joined the group of leaders or church council of our imaginary downtown church (page 27). What changes would you want to propose in order to develop a better balance between concern for truth and love?

5. 'To practise love is to reflect the character and concerns of God as he has shown himself to us in Jesus.' Can you suggest any particular ways in which God may be prompting your church to 'practise love'?

To the angel of the church in Smyrna write: These are the words of him who is the First and the Last, who died and came to life again. I know your afflictions and your poverty — yet you are rich! I know the slander of those who say they are Jews and are not, but are a synagogue of Satan. Do not be afraid of what you are about to suffer. I tell you, the devil will put some of you in prison to test you, and you will suffer persecution for ten days. Be faithful, even to the point of death, and I will give you the crown of life.

He who has an ear, let him hear what the Spirit says to the churches. He who overcomes will not be hurt at all by the second death.

Revelation 2:8–11

CHAPTER 3

The Church at Smyrna –
persecuted but rich

(Revelation 2:8–11)

The next port of call for John's messenger is thirty-five miles to the north. If Ephesus was the market place of Asia Minor, Smyrna was described as its 'ornament'. Aelius Aristides, a second century orator who lived in Smyrna, spoke of 'the grace which extends over every part of it like a rainbow, and the brightness which reaches up towards the skies, like the glitter of the bronze of armour in Homer's epics'. Homer, author of the epic poems *The Iliad* and *The Odyssey*, was to the Greeks what Shakespeare is to the English, and Smyrna was his Stratford-upon-Avon.

Its importance as a city derived from its secure harbour at the eastern end of a narrow gulf on the Aegean coastline. Traders from Mesopotamia and the east brought their goods to it along the Golden Way, a major route which passed through Sardis and the Hermus Valley. Smyrna was home to more than 100,000 people. Its buildings rose up from the harbour, filling the lower slopes of Mount Pagus. The appearance of the buildings on its summit, viewed from a distance, gave rise to its nickname 'the crown of Smyrna'.

The first and the last

Presumably the church in Smyrna had been founded through Christian witness stemming from Ephesus. For Luke tells us that through Paul's mission in Ephesus 'all the Jews and Greeks who lived in the province of Asia heard the word of the Lord' (Acts 19:10). But the Lord has no criticism for the daughter church like that which he launched on Ephesus. Smyrna (now called Izmir) is in fact the only church of the seven which has never died out. Facing persecution and poverty, she is reminded who it is who addresses her: he is 'the First and the Last, who died and came to life again' (verse 8).

The people of Smyrna knew about death and resurrection. For their city had been destroyed about 600 BC, and then re-established on a new site three hundred years later. It was, said Aristides, like a phoenix – the mythical bird which was supposed at the end of its life to burn itself on a funeral pyre and rise renewed from its own ashes.

The phoenix also appears in early Christian art as a symbol of Christ's resurrection. Christians at Smyrna serve a Lord whose death was not the end, but the source of life for all who trust in him. He has this power over death because he is 'the First and the Last'. In the Old Testament this is a title of God himself (Is. 44:6; 48:12). He is the source and the goal of everything that exists. Nothing in the end can frustrate his loving purpose for the world. There could hardly be a more striking way of underlining the supremacy of Christ over everything that threatens his people. Why then does he not use his supremacy to remove the suffering and the threat of death? That is a question to which we must return after we have looked at what the church at Smyrna was actually facing.

'I know your afflictions and your poverty' (verse 9). In a prosperous town, the poverty of Christians was probably a direct result of other people's hostility towards them. Perhaps their property had been attacked by mobs. Perhaps it was hard for them to get work because they were unwilling to compromise with pagan standards, or because employers viewed them with suspicion.

'Yet you are rich!' (verse 9). Poor and battered they may be, but they are rich in everything that really matters. How different from the self-satisfied church of Laodicea, whose supposed wealth Christ will prick like a soap-bubble (3:17-18). For countless Christians today living under oppressive regimes, their faith keeps them at the back of the queue for jobs, deprives them of opportunities for higher education, and ensures their continuing poverty. But are they *really* poorer than those who have become comfortable under the stupefying effects of affluence?

The synagogue of Satan

The real problem, however, comes from Jews in Smyrna. 'I know the slander of those who say they are Jews and are

not, but are a synagogue of Satan' (verse 9). Why should
Jesus' followers provoke slanderous attacks by Jews? Why
should John be so provocative as to call them a synagogue,
not of God, but of Satan?

We know from the Acts of the Apostles that Jews often
stirred up opposition to the new message. This was partly
because the Christians were finding fertile ground for their
mission among Gentile 'Godfearers' who were attracted to
the Jewish faith and had attached themselves to the
synagogues. Thus Jews felt that members of their own congregations were being 'stolen' by the new sect.

Although the Roman authorities at first had made no distinction between Jews and Christians, two events created a
clear division between the two communities. In AD 64 there
was a great fire in Rome, which critics of the emperor Nero
suspected him of starting in order to clear ground for a grand
rebuilding programme. In order to divert the charge away
from himself he accused the Christians of arson and persecuted them brutally. From that time Christians were
identified as a group distinct from the Jews.

Secondly, the arrival in Asia of Jewish refugees from
Palestine during the Jewish war against Rome (AD 66-70)
intensified bitterness against Christians. For Christians in
Palestine had refused to identify with the Jewish Revolt, and
had understood the destruction of the temple as God's
judgment on Judaism's failure to recognize Jesus as Messiah.
After the war Judaism began to close ranks and to exclude
from the synagogues all heretics, especially Christians.

Under Domitian, the requirement that Jews should pay a
tax to Jupiter's temple in Rome was strictly enforced, even

on Jews who had ceased to practise their religion, and on
non-Jews who followed a Jewish way of life. Christians, of
course, might be caught on either count.

Here, then, is rich potential for suspicion and bitter hostility between Jews and Christians. Ever since the war of
AD 66–70, Jews feel vulnerable. They have lost some of the
protection previously enjoyed under Roman law. Some are
tempted to protect their own position by informing
against Christians who haven't paid their temple-tax or
who might be suspected of anti-Roman tendencies. They
are resentful of this new heresy which has stolen some of
their own Gentile adherents and has brought them nothing but trouble. Christians are vulnerable too. They can no
longer 'hide' under the protection of Judaism, because Jews
will acknowledge them no longer. Yet if they distance
themselves from Judaism and proclaim their distinctive-
ness, they risk drawing attention to themselves and being
accused of belonging to an unauthorized religion. So the
temptation is to go soft on their witness, to melt into the
background. For some this might mean following a Jewish
lifestyle and hoping not to be recognized as different. For
others, perhaps, the safest thing was to merge into pagan
society.

We should never underestimate the pressure on
Christians to merge into the background, to adopt the
lifestyle of the surrounding culture in order to avoid
ridicule or hostility. Whether they are converts from
Hinduism, young people in secondary school or young pro-
fessionals in the City, they need all the help they can get to
face the risks of living differently.

Jewish people in Smyrna are 'a synagogue of Satan' because they are abusing the followers of Jesus and putting their lives in danger. They 'say they are Jews and are not' because, though they are Jews by race, they have not responded to Jesus as God's Messiah. The true people of God, as the New Testament constantly claims, is not an ethnic group but a spiritual nation consisting of people who may be Jewish or Gentile by race. As Paul had written to Gentiles at Ephesus: 'Now in Christ Jesus you who once were far away have been brought near through the blood of Christ... He came and preached peace to you who were far away and peace to those who were near. For through him we both have access to the Father by one Spirit' (Eph. 2:13, 17–18).

Jesus the Messiah

This uncompromising message to Smyrna provokes awkward questions. Is it not arrogant for Christians to imagine that we have the whole truth and that Jews can be dismissed as misguided followers of an outdated faith? It may be all right for missionaries to bring the gospel to people of primitive and superstitious religions, or even to challenge the great world faiths at points where they seem to be inadequate. But can it be right to confront directly the faith from which Christianity came? Did not the first Christians themselves believe that 'the God of Abraham and Isaac and Jacob' is also 'the God and Father of our Lord Jesus Christ'? And of course our unease about Christian mission to Jews is multiplied a thousandfold by our embarrassment at hundreds of years of Christian persecution of Jews.

To give up on Christian witness to Jews may seem prudent, charitable, logical. But it would be a case of sawing off the branch on which we sit. The foundation of the Christian faith, the one factor which brought it into existence in the first place, is the belief that Jesus came as the Messiah promised to Israel. Affirm that Jesus is the Messiah, and you are inevitably committed to sharing that belief with Jews whose Messiah he came to be. Deny that he is the Messiah, and there is no more reason for Christianity to exist. If Jesus is not the Messiah of the Jews, he cannot be my Saviour or the Saviour of the world.

We cannot give up the conviction shared by John and all the New Testament writers that Jesus is the climax of Judaism. There is a sense in which people who are Jewish by race need to discover Jesus' messiahship if they are to keep up with God's purpose for his people and enjoy the benefits of being his children. But witness to this truth does not have to be arrogant or aggressive. It must be sensitive, always conscious that for centuries Jews have been oppressed by so-called Christian civilizations.

In that case, can the strong language about the 'synagogue of Satan' be excused? Isn't it just the kind of anti-Semitism which we need to get rid of? Before we dismiss such language, we should recognize it as the language of one who is himself a Jew. And he is writing to fellow-Christians, a mixture of Jews and Gentiles, whose faith is being tested to the limit by the hostility of their Jewish contemporaries. It is the language of a man troubled by the failure of his own people to receive the Messiah whom God has sent to them. So it is quite different from anti-Semitism as we know it, which arises from racial hatred and nationalistic contempt for others.

A taste of suffering

The persecution which the church now faces will be costly for some. 'The devil will put some of you in prison to test you, and you will suffer persecution for ten days' (verse 10). Imprisonment in the Roman world was not itself a punishment but simply a way of keeping people under guard while they awaited sentence. The punishment itself will be 'persecution for ten days'. which will lead some 'to the point of death'. The number of days here may recall the language found in inscriptions at Smyrna announcing athletic games and gladiatorial contests, for which the city was famous. Some of Smyrna's Christians might be called on to appear as victims of gladiators' swords or as fodder for wild animals at a forthcoming festival – the 'ten-day games'.

There is no promise of escape from suffering, though there is a hint as to where it comes from. It comes from *the devil*, and is therefore part of the battle which rages between good and evil, between the power of God and the forces seeking to frustrate him. Yet at the same time God uses it to test and refine his servants' faith. God's people are called not to avoid suffering, not even to understand it, but to suffer with their Lord in order to share his glory. The one who says, 'Do not be afraid" (verse 10), is the Lord whose own suffering opened the way to life.

In the age-long battle between God and Satan, God knows no other victory and needs no other victory than that which is won by the Cross of Christ, faithfully proclaimed to the world by the martyr witness of his church.

George B. Caird

So when people say in the face of suffering or catastrophe, 'Why doesn't God *do* something?', John has the hint of an answer. It is that God shows himself not normally in acts of dramatic power, like Zeus hurling thunderbolts from the heavens, but in the suffering itself. Christ won his victory over evil by giving himself to suffering in such a way as to draw its sting. The whole story of God's dealings with the world is cross-shaped. And when people offer their suffering to him rather than railing bitterly about it, he uses it for the healing of the world.

I know someone who, years ago, lost his job after he was falsely accused of misconduct. The memory of it still brings tears to his eyes. He began a new life in another country and began to work for the rehabilitation of young people severely damaged physically and emotionally by the oppression of a brutal regime. His own experience of rejection and injustice enabled him, as nothing else could, to sympathize with those young people and to bring them hope and healing.

One man's response to John's message

Probably among the congregation who received this letter was a young man named Polycarp, who later became famous as bishop of Smyrna and as a martyr. When he died as an old man in AD 156 he was revered as the last link with those who had known Jesus during his earthly life, for he had sat at the feet of the apostle John. The account of his death by an eyewitness tells how, during an outbreak of anti-Christian activity in the province of Asia, the mob cried out for Polycarp's blood.

A police squad was sent to fetch him and the police commissioner, probably wishing to spare the old man the indignities ahead, asked, 'What harm is there in just saying "Caesar is Lord" and offering incense, when it will save your life?'

Polycarp refused his advice, and was taken to the arena where the provincial governor himself tried to persuade him to renounce his faith.

'Have some respect for your age,' he said. 'Swear an oath by the divinity of Caesar, repent and say, "Down with the atheists!"'

By 'atheists', of course, the governor meant the Christians, but Polycarp waved his hand towards the seething crowd in the arena and said, 'Down with the atheists!'

The governor pressed him further: 'Take the oath and I will let you go. Revile your Christ.'

Polycarp then made his memorable reply: 'Eighty-six years I have served him, and he has done me no wrong. How then can I blaspheme my King and Saviour?'

Further argument proved fruitless. Polycarp was threatened with being thrown to wild beasts but eventually it was decided to burn him to death. The crowd, including Jews whose hostility to Christians evidently continued, gathered firewood, and Polycarp was chained to the stake. His final words were a prayer:

> *O Lord God Almighty, Father of your blessed and beloved Son Jesus Christ, through whom we have been given knowledge of yourself..., I bless you for granting this day and hour that I may be numbered among the martyrs, to share the cup of your Messiah and to rise again to eternal life....*

Faithful till death

Smyrna knew all about faithfulness. For nearly three hundred years it had been a loyal ally of Rome. In 195 BC it had built the first temple ever to be dedicated to the city of Rome, and since AD 26, when a temple to the emperor was built, it had been an important centre of emperor worship. But faithfulness to the King of kings brings a reward far greater than anything Rome can offer. Alluding to the 'crown of Smyrna' as well as to the crown won by an athlete, Jesus says: 'I will give you the crown of life.... He who overcomes will not be hurt at all by the second death' (verses 10–11). The persecutors may kill people's bodies but they have no power to impose the death of separation from God.

One of the victims of Idi Amin's tyranny in Uganda in the 1970s was Archbishop Janani Luwum, whose quiet but firm opposition to Amin's policies became more than the dictator could stomach. When he was summoned for a meeting with the President his wife tried to dissuade him from going. 'I will go', he replied. 'Even if he kills me, my blood will save the nation.' And when on 16th February 1977 trumped-up charges were read out at a staged trial, he whispered to a fellow-bishop, 'They are going to kill me. I am not afraid.' Later the same day he was shot.

And yet those of us who do not face the extreme threat experienced by those Christian in Uganda and John's friends in Smyrna perhaps need to hear another message. Many people are more likely to deny their faith through fear of being laughed at than through fear of the firing squad. The apostle Peter eventually faced martyrdom by crucifixion. Yet he had earlier denied his Lord when stung by a mocking remark (Mk. 14:66-72). But the Lord who stands by those who die out of loyalty to him, stands by each of us in our daily struggle to represent him faithfully in the world.

Facing opposition

Some Christians have to face constant opposition from the state authorities or from other religious groups, from people at work or within their own families. Some even find their lives in danger. For all of us there are periods when our faith is severely tested. How can we survive such pressure?

● Remember the words of the risen Christ: 'I know your afflictions' (Rev. 2:9). Our situation does not catch him by surprise.

● Remember that Jesus not only knows but shares our suffering. At the heart of Christianity is the cross which tells
us that God has entered a suffering world, to suffer for us
and with us. In the library of Corpus Christi College,
Cambridge is a rather dirty-looking Bible which
belonged to Thomas Bilney, one of the minor characters
of the English Reformation in the sixteenth century. He
was no great hero and sometimes wavered in his faith.
But in the end he was burnt at the stake for his commitment to the gospel. In his Bible the verses which
comforted him in his last days are heavily marked in ink:

> *Fear not, for I have redeemed you;*
> *I have called you by name; you are mine....*
> *When you walk through the fire you will not be burned;*
> *the flames will not set you ablaze.*
> *For I am the Lord, your God, the Holy One of Israel, your Saviour.*
> Isaiah 43:1-3

● Give and receive encouragement from other Christians.
'Remember those in prison as if you were their fellow-
prisoners, and those who are ill-treated as if you
yourselves were suffering' (Heb. 13:3). 'Carry each other's
burdens, and in this way you will fulfil the law of Christ'
(Gal. 6:2).

● Take encouragement from the words of Jesus, who lived
as he taught: 'Bless those who curse you, pray for those
who ill-treat you' (Lk. 6:28). By an extraordinary irony of
human experience it is often those who have suffered

greatly who are most able to forgive. In 1943 Etty
Hillesum, a Dutch Jew, was taken with her family to
Auschwitz, where they all met their deaths. Despite the
horror of the suffering she never gave in to hate. In her
diary she commented how cruel and merciless the Nazis
were, adding, 'We must be all the more merciful
ourselves.'

● Pray for strength not to provoke by argument those who
oppose you, but to live a deeply Christian life. 'Make
every effort to live in peace with everyone and to be
holy' (Rom. 12:14). 'Always be prepared to give an
answer to everyone who asks you to give the reason for
the hope that you have. But do this with gentleness and
respect, keeping a clear conscience, so that those who
speak maliciously against your good behaviour in Christ
may be ashamed of their slander' (1 Pet. 3:15-16).

● Remember that for most of us the Christian life is a
marathon race, not a sprint. There is no quick escape
from hardship. There is what has been called 'a long obedience in the same direction'. Wang Mingdao, a Chinese
Christian leader imprisoned for twenty-three years after
the Communists came to power, was sustained by the
convictions which he had earlier taught to others:

To maintain one's faith while enduring insults and suffering perse-
cution for a prolonged period is more difficult than standing for the
truth by laying down one's life. In order to achieve the latter it is
necessary only to be strong and courageous for one day. But to

endure ridicule, hostility and persecution constantly — to reproduce the strength and courage of one day for months or years or even tens of years — that requires even greater faith and courage and an even higher level of   obedience.

And he clung to the words of Jesus:

'Blessed are you when people insult you, persecute you and falsely say all kinds of evil against you because of me. Rejoice and be glad, because great is your reward in heaven, for in the same way they persecuted the prophets who were before you.'

Matthew 5:11–12

Questions for reflection and discussion

1. What particularly in this chapter has helped you or made you think?

2. 'They need all the help they can get to face the risks of living differently' (page 41). Think of some of the people in your church who face particular pressures because they work in an environment which is hostile to Christian values. How can the church strengthen and support them?

3. 'If Jesus is not the Messiah of the Jews, he cannot be my Saviour or the Saviour of the world' (page 43). Do you agree? If so, how can Christian witness to Jews be expressed without appearing insensitive to the Jewish memory of oppression from Christian civilizations?

4. Can you suggest examples from your experience of how the suffering of Christians has been transformed by the sense of God's involvement in it?

5. 'I know your afflictions and your poverty – yet you are rich!' (Revelation 2:9). What kinds of riches do you think these words refer to? You may like to share with each other your thoughts about how Christ has enriched your own experience, and then make these thoughts the basis of prayers of thanksgiving.

To the angel of the church in Pergamum write: These are the words of him who has the sharp, double-edged sword. I know where you live — where Satan has his throne. Yet you remain true to my name. You did not renounce your faith in me, even in the days of Antipas, my faithful witness, who was put to death in your city — where Satan lives.

Nevertheless, I have a few things against you: You have people there who hold to the teaching of Balaam, who taught Balak to entice the Israelites to sin by eating food sacrificed to idols and by committing sexual immorality. Likewise you also have those who hold to the teaching of the Nicolaitans. Repent therefore! Otherwise, I will soon come to you and will fight against them with the sword of my mouth.

He who has an ear, let him hear what the Spirit says to the churches. To him who overcomes, I will give some of the hidden manna. I will also give him a white stone with a new name written on it, known only to him who receives it.

Revelation 2:12–17

CHAPTER 4

The Church at Pergamum – loyal yet compromised

(Revelation 2:12–17)

The messenger must travel sixty-five miles to Pergamum, capital of the Roman province of Asia. While most of its 120,000 inhabitants lived in the lower city towards the river Caicus, town planners made the most of its spectacular granite acropolis, which rises three hundred metres above the valley. Here were temples of Demeter and Athena, Hera and Zeus. Gods of every kind had their worshippers in Pergamum. And none was more popular than Asclepius the god of healing, whose huge sanctuary south of the city was one of the most famous healing centres in the ancient world. Here people came from near and far to try its spa waters and to seek a miracle from the god. But the greatest threat to the young church came from another form of worship.

Satan's throne

As the political capital of the province of Asia, Pergamum was the centre of emperor-worship. In 29 BC the first emperor Augustus allowed the building of a temple dedicated to Rome and to himself. What began harmlessly enough as a province's way of expressing its loyalty to Rome, could be made into a ruthless test of political conformity. Conscientious refusal to take part in worship of the emperor could be interpreted as treason by a regime intent on suppressing dangerous ideas. Domitian, with his demand to be worshipped as 'lord and god', seemed to herald the arrival of just such a regime. And now one Christian, Antipas, has been killed for maintaining his faith (verse 13). Perhaps the authorities had decided to make an example of him in order to weaken the resolve of other Christians. But because of his loyalty to Christ he now bears the same title as his Lord: 'faithful witness' (verse 13; compare 1:5).

Though 'Satan's throne' (verse 13) has sometimes been identified with the altar of Zeus or with the temple of Asclepius, it seems most likely that this ominous phrase refers to emperor-worship and all that it might imply for John's readers. He sees Rome and its abuse of power as a terrifying expression of evil, the very opposite of God's loving and creative purpose.

In each of the other six letters Christ says to the church, 'I know your *deeds.*' To Pergamum he says, 'I know *where you live* – where Satan has his throne' (verse 13). In other words, he understands their situation, he knows the pressures they have to bear. And he commends them for holding fast. The word 'live' suggests permanent residence. The church lives where Satan lives, and it has no right to escape. It is there in the darkness to bear witness to the light, costly though that may be.

Many churches today which fight their battle in hard places must be tempted to look for a way out, a way of easing the strain. But Christ has them there for a purpose. He understands how they feel, and he reminds them that he 'has the sharp, double-edged sword' (verse 12).

This description of Christ, echoing the vision in Revelation 1:16, is loaded with irony. The proconsul, or governor, of the Roman province of Asia had almost unlimited power. The death of Antipas was just one instance of his power at work. And the sword was the symbol of his rule. But in the end his power is no match for the sword which comes from the mouth of Christ (1:16) – his word which will finally bring God's purpose to its goal. 'Out of his mouth came a sharp sword with which to strike down the nations. He will rule them with an iron sceptre. He treads the wine-press of the fury of the wrath of God Almighty' (Rev. 19:15).

In a world of brute force, it is some comfort to know that what counts most in the end is not the size of a nation's army or the mega-tonnage of its bombs, but the word of the crucified Man. In human terms the story of Jesus is the story of a wise man crushed by political force. From God's view-point it is the most powerful, the most creative event in all human history.

Accusation

The word of Christ cuts deep also among his own people.

> *I have a few things against you: You have people there who hold to the teaching of Balaam, who taught Balak to entice the Israelites to sin by eating food sacrificed to idols and by committing sexual immorality. Likewise you also have those who hold to the teaching of the Nicolaitans.*
>
> Revelation 2:14–15

Whereas the church at Ephesus was guilty of a loveless resistance to the teaching of the Nicolaitans, the church at Pergamum is accused of allowing this group to prosper within its fellowship. The line is so fine between tolerance and intolerance, between loving correction of false teaching and an uncritical acceptance of new ideas! The letter to Ephesus commended careful testing to check whether a new teaching conforms to the truth revealed in Jesus (2:2). This letter highlights the need to test *ourselves*, to see whether we are keeping alert to the danger of being influenced by false teachings.

John takes an excursion into Jewish tradition to explain the Nicolaitans' teaching further. After Balak king of Moab had tried without success to persuade Balaam to curse the Israelites during their journey from Egypt (Num. 22–24), the Israelite men began to have intercourse with Moabite women, to eat their sacrificed animals and to worship their gods (Num. 25:1). Jewish tradition, with the help of Numbers 31:16, explained that it was on Balaam's advice that Balak sent Moabite women to seduce the men of Israel into this abandonment of moral and religious purity. So Balaam was remembered in Jewish thought as the originator of religious syncretism – that is, the compromising of one's own faith by mixing it with ideas and practices from other faiths.

Now the Nicolaitans are leading God's people in the same direction. The 'apostolic decree' issued by the Council of Jerusalem in AD 49 had forbidden sexual immorality and the eating of food sacrificed to idols (Acts 15:20). In Gentile cities most meat sold in the markets was surplus from pagan temples where it had been killed for sacrifice to the gods. And meat-eating was a main attraction at the special dinners often held at these temples by the trade-guilds which were a common feature of city life. There were guilds of silver-smiths, singers, bakers, potters and numerous other crafts.

Paul had reckoned that Christians could eat meat bought in the market, since it could not be contaminated by association with idols who don't really exist anyway. But they should not eat meals in the temples because that would involve them in worship of false gods (1 Cor. 8–10). But the Nicolaitans were not impressed by such views. Sexual immorality, too, presented no problem to them. Indeed, they vigorously defended it in the name of 'Christian freedom'.

The Christian and society

It may surprise us that people who claimed to be Christian could take such a stance. But perhaps the issue was not so clear-cut to some of the church at Pergamum. Imagine a conversation between Hermas and his wife Mary when he arrives home late one night from the annual dinner of the Clothworkers' Guild.

Mary   Was it a good do, Hermas?

Hermas Yes, dear, I reckon the best yet. The meal was fantastic, the roast suckling-pig was out of this world, and the dancing girls were... Well, you wouldn't want to know about them, would you?

Mary   Hermas, I've been thinking while you were out. Do you think you ought to go to these dinners? It doesn't seem right to me that you go and sit in the temple of Dionysus while they make sacrifices to the god, all for the sake of keeping in with the other clothworkers.

Hermas But, don't you realize, if I don't pull my weight in the Clothworkers' Guild I'll be out of a job. What would you and the children do then? Anyway, you're being far too sensitive. You know and I know that Dionysus doesn't really exist. We don't take these sacrifices seriously. It's just a bit of harmless tradition.

Mary   But don't you have to drink a toast or something to the emperor, and call him 'lord and god'? If you call that harmless tradition I call it blasphemy.

Hermas Oh Mary, don't you remember that Jesus himself told us to pay Caesar what belongs to Caesar, and that the Roman authorities are there by God's permission? I was able to say something in my speech about the Christian responsibility to the state. But if you had your way we might as well all become hermits, and there'd be no Christian witness at all, would there?

Mary   Well, perhaps, but it still doesn't seem right. I thought being a follower of Jesus meant being prepared to take a stand against all this worship of false gods, even if we have to suffer for it. I mean, Jesus didn't exactly go sucking up to those high-and-mighty Romans so that he could make a good impression on them, did he?

Hermas   Maybe not, but he did go to parties with the sort of folk that religious people wouldn't touch with a bargepole, sinners and what have you.

Mary   And that brings me to another point. Where were you the night before last? You didn't know I saw you coming back from *that* part of town at five o'clock in the morning, did you? How long am I supposed to put up with this sort of behaviour?

Hermas   Mary, I haven't stopped caring about you. You're the only woman that matters to me. But you're a bit old-fashioned to tell me off over a bit of pleasure. Christ has set us free to do anything. To go with a prostitute doesn't affect me any more than I'm affected by whether I eat beef or cauliflower. What we do with our bodies doesn't affect the salvation of our souls. That's the great thing about being a Christian – freedom from all the old rules, freedom to be yourself...'

Actually, the conversation would have been far less calm and logical than that, because Hermas was probably suffering the effects of the Philadelphian wine he enjoyed at the dinner. But such arguments must have gone on in places like Pergamum. We know that they went on in Corinth, because 1 Corinthians 6:12-20 shows Paul responding to someone who has offered just the same arguments as Hermas. But the important thing is this: according to the Lord of the church, Mary is right, and Hermas has distorted the gospel. He has allowed his thinking to be shaped more by the surrounding society than by Christ.

How compromise takes place

The church at Pergamum tolerated compromise with the surrounding society. We ourselves may accept compromise in a thousand ways. Our temperaments, our experience of life and our personal convictions will help to determine the points at which we refuse to compromise, and those at which we compromise our faith without really noticing. Christians today may imitate the weakness of the church at Pergamum in many ways. Take time now to reflect on which ones of the following list may be true of you. Which might be true of your church situation?

We are like the church at Pergamum when we:

- Are more concerned to be popular than to be faithful to Christ;

- expect to find glory without suffering, birth without pain;

- accept without question the values which dominate our society – for example, the expectation of an ever-increasing standard of living, whatever implications this may have for other people or other nations;

- do something simply because 'everybody does it';

- give space to the idea that Jesus is only one of many possible ways to God;

- surrender to the common assumption that God may receive attention on Sundays, but has little to do with our lives from Monday to Saturday;

- allow people to kid us that religion is a private matter, not to be discussed or argued about, and certainly not to be related to everyday life or to business or political affairs;

- look to Jesus simply as a personal source of help and encouragement, rather than as the Lord of creation who has a purpose for the whole world and calls us to be involved in that purpose;

● fail to see how revolutionary the Sermon on the Mount
(Mt. 5–7) is meant to be when it is actually allowed to
mould our vision of what our own lives and our society
might become.

The Christ who spoke to the seven churches challenges
us to discover our own compromises and to allow him
to transform our thinking and our actions. 'Let anyone
who has an ear listen to what the Spirit is saying to the
churches.'

Confronting un-Christian behaviour

When we have heard Christ's exposure of our compromises there is only one way forward: 'Repent therefore!
Otherwise, I will soon come to you and will fight against
them with the sword of my mouth' (verse 16). The whole
church is called to repent. It has been too tolerant of the
Nicolaitans' compromise with emperor-worship and abuse
of Christian freedom. It has failed to discern the limits of
authentic Christian behaviour. And so its witness to the
world is hopelessly blurred.

When should a church take a firm stand against attitudes
and practices which seem questionable to most of its members? When should it accept variant lifestyles as a proper
expression of Christian diversity? Many churches, for example, accept that within their membership people may hold
different convictions about war and pacifism, or the use of
alcohol. Yet they may not accept that Christian diversity can

include people who have adopted a homosexual lifestyle. On what grounds is such a distinction made?

These are difficult questions, and Christians will often disagree about the answers. They may disagree because they give differing weight to the authority of the Bible. They may disagree because some look to their church leadership for a definite 'line' on a particular controversial issue, while others allow more freedom to the individual Christian conscience. Some, who stress the importance of law in the Bible, will want rules to be laid down. Others will argue that the generous grace of God makes it inappropriate to lay down rules which will create barriers between those who conform and those who do not.

Against such a background, what I say here may not be to everyone's taste. But a church needs some guidelines for deciding where the boundaries of acceptable behaviour lie, and how it should respond to those who overstep the boundary. Readers may wish to add to or alter the following guidelines, but if so they should be able to give reasons for their views.

● We must recognize that the defining of acceptable limits of behaviour is not inconsistent with the gospel of forgiveness for all. Paul, who proclaimed God's generosity over against any idea that salvation could be gained by keeping rules, nevertheless summarized various kinds of behaviour which simply can't be squared with faith in Jesus (1 Cor. 6:9-10; Gal. 5:19-21). Jesus, who declared God's magnificent forgiveness to sinners, made great demands on his followers. The pattern is shown in his encounter with the

woman caught in adultery: 'Neither do I condemn you...
Go now and leave your life of sin' (Jn. 8:11).

● The church must seek to maintain among its members a
lifestyle which reflects Christ's character. This will involve
teaching, encouragement and discipline of members who
live in open contradiction of that standard.

● The purpose of discipline in the church is not merely to
maintain purity but to win the offender to a fuller life in
Christ (Mat. 18:15; Gal. 6:1).

● If the Bible condemns with a consistent voice a particular
practice (for instance, financial deceit or sexual unfaithfulness)
a church should be willing to demonstrate its disapproval.

● On matters where the Bible speaks with varying voices
(for example, war and pacifism) or does not speak explic-
itly at all (for example, the ethics of advertising), a church
is wise not to lay down rules.

● When a particular kind of behaviour by Christians is
liable to bring the gospel into disrepute among non-
Christians, the church must act firmly. This is the
principle at work in 1 Corinthians 5, where Paul confronts immorality 'of a kind that does not occur even
among pagans' (1 Cor. 5:1).

● The church must try to get over its long-standing obses-
sion with sexual sins, as though they were somehow

more serious than others. Paul's warnings set sexual immorality alongside such sins as idolatry, jealousy, greed and selfish ambition (Gal. 5:19-21; Eph. 5:5-6). There may be need for teaching and discipline in those areas too.

● A procedure for exercising discipline is suggested in Matthew 18:15-17. The offender is first to be challenged privately. The matter will concern the larger church community – and not simply an individual church leader – only if there is no repentance after this first approach. They will act prayerfully and carefully together, demonstrating pastoral support as well as concern to uphold the church's standards. They may perhaps entrust such a task to a representative group of mature Christians.

● In considering how to take action over an offender, a church must think about the *direction* of a person's life. For instance, if a young couple who live together unmarried come to experience the love of Christ and want to join the church, it would be quite wrong for the church to jump down their throats for 'living in sin'. It should expect that its teaching and its prayer will bring them to a change of heart. They are moving in the right direction. But if the churchwarden or a senior deacon embezzles church funds they should be disciplined. They ought to know better.

● The church must maintain a sense of proportion, even a sense of humour, in all this. No amount of discipline will make a perfect church, and Jesus' parable of the wheat and the tares suggests that this should not surprise us (Mt. 13:24-30, 36-43).

● When someone responds to discipline with repentance they must be welcomed generously, not grudgingly. God welcomes them without reservation, and the church has no business acting otherwise (Mt. 18:10-14).

Hidden manna and a white stone

The final promise is expressed in words specially fitting for Pergamum. 'To him who overcomes, I will give some of the hidden manna. I will also give him a white stone with a new name written on it, known only to him who receives it' (verse 17). There was a Jewish tradition that a sample of the manna given to the Israelites on their wilderness journey from Egypt (Ex. 16:32-34) had been hidden until the coming of the Messiah, when it would be food for the saints. So the message is this: just as ancient Israel, tempted by Balaam, was fed by manna, so the true Israel of John's day, after resisting the temptations offered by the Nicolaitans, will be fed by heavenly bread. Those who refuse to seek earthly safety by being at home in the banquets of the world will find themselves at home at the feast-table of the Messiah.

The white stone may contain several allusions. Jurors used to give a stone to a man at the end of his trial – white indicating 'not guilty', black for 'guilty'. If this were in mind, it would be a message of assurance that the church which remains faithful is held firm in God's love. Or it may allude to the custom of using white stones as admission tickets to public festivals. There is certain admission to the manna-feast for 'him who overcomes'.

And the new name? Because it is 'known only to him who receives it' it remains something of a mystery! But it expresses the new and secure relationship between Christ and the Christian. People who are close to each other sometimes use private names, terms of endearment, which no one else knows. If I receive from Christ's hand a white stone inscribed with a secret new name, I am known and loved so much by him that nothing can tear me from his grip.

The church at Pergamum, then, was something of a mixture. Their commitment to Christ had already been severely tested, and one of them had paid with his life. Yet some had adopted an understanding of 'Christian freedom' which made them little different from the surrounding society. And the church as a whole, accepting this state of affairs, had lost the cutting edge of its witness.

Perhaps when we look at ourselves this mixture is not so strange as it at first appears. If faced with a clear-cut choice, whether to remain true to Christ or renounce him to save our skin, we might find within us the strength to face the firing squad. But when persecution is remote, we may all too easily conform to the prevailing assumptions and lifestyles of our society. We may then become, instead of guides to point others to the right road, simply a well-disguised group of travellers, indistinguishable from the crowd.

Questions for reflection and discussion

1. What particularly in this chapter has helped you or made you think?

2. Review the examples of compromise which are suggested on pages 62-4. Which of them are the most liable to affect you or your church? How can we help each other to resist them?

3. In your experience, is the church too tough or too soft about applying discipline to its members? What guidelines for discipline are appropriate, and what pitfalls are to be avoided?

4. 'We may become ... simply a well-disguised group of travellers, indistinguishable from the crowd' (page 69). Do you agree? Can you suggest ways in which Christians can be seen to be different from the crowd?

To the angel of the church in Thyatira write: These are the words of the Son of God, whose eyes are like blazing fire and whose feet are like burnished bronze. I know your deeds, your love and faith, your service and perseverance, and that you are now doing more than you did at first.

Nevertheless, I have this against you: You tolerate that woman Jezebel, who calls herself a prophetess. By her teaching she misleads my servants into sexual immorality and the eating of food sacrificed to idols. I have given her time to repent of her immorality, but she is unwilling. So I will cast her on a bed of suffering, and I will make those who commit adultery with her suffer intensely, unless they repent of her ways. I will strike her children dead. Then all the churches will know that I am he who searches hearts and minds, and I will repay each of you according to your deeds. Now I say to the rest of you in Thyatira, to you who do not hold to her teaching and have not learned Satan's so-called deep secrets (I will not impose any other burden on you): Only hold on to what you have until I come.

To him who overcomes and does my will to the end, I will give authority over the nations —

'He will rule them with an iron sceptre;
he will dash them to pieces like pottery' —

just as I have received authority from my Father. I will also give him the morning star. He who has an ear, let him hear what the Spirit says to the churches.

Revelation 2:18–29

CHAPTER 5

The Church at Thyatira – split by false teaching

(Revelation 2:18–29)

Thyatira lay in a gentle vale thirty-five miles south-east of Pergamum. Unlike Pergamum it had no imposing acropolis, no colourful history with which to impress. But its position on the imperial post-route made it a thriving centre of trade. One product which it traded with great success was purple cloth, dyed with pigment from the root of the local madder plant. Lydia, Paul's first convert in Europe, was a dealer in purple fabric who had gone to Philippi from Thyatira, perhaps as overseas agent of a company exporting the cloth to new markets (Acts 16:11–15).

There is no sign here of the political oppression caused by the prominence of the emperor-cult at Pergamum. But the church faces other pressures similar to those in the province's capital. For here the trade-guilds are particularly active. There are guilds of tailors, bakers, tanners, potters, linen-workers, wool-merchants, dyers, slave-traders and coppersmiths. So the same dilemmas come up again. Can Christians with a clear conscience take part in the life of a

trade-guild, or will that inevitably compromise their obedience to the one true God? Can they risk the social
rejection which may result from opting out of the guild for
conscience's sake?

At Pergamum some Christian's *lives* were threatened
by the emperor-cult. At Thyatira their *livelihood* is threatened by the trade-guilds. And perhaps it is easier to
recognize and resist the pressure of a political regime than
the pressure that comes from social and economic forces.

The God who sees

The pressures are clear to the one who speaks to the church
at Thyatira. He is 'the Son of God, whose eyes are like blazing fire, and whose feet are like burnished bronze' (verse
18). His eyes see through all our excuses, all our attempts to
justify why we have chosen the less demanding path rather
than the awkward route of costly obedience.

The word for 'burnished bronze' occurs only here in
Greek literature, and John uses it because it has special associations for his readers. The coppersmiths of Thyatira had
developed a sophisticated technique for making a particularly fine kind of brass, an alloy of copper and zinc which
involved the distillation of zinc to remove impurities. The
fact that the word they used for it does not appear in other
Greek writings suggests that its manufacture was a secret
closely guarded by the coppersmiths' guild. But for John it
enhances the picture of the Son of God as the church's true
defender against all that threatens it. He is irresistibly

clothed in armour flashing like the refined metal from the furnaces of the town.

He is generous in his praise for a church which has refused to seek survival by pulling up the drawbridge against a hostile world. It is full of loving actions, faithfulness towards God, service towards other people, and endurance in the face of obstacles provided by the world (verse 19). And, unlike the church at Ephesus whose love has waned (2:4), it continues to grow in these Christ-like qualities: 'You are now doing more than you did at first' (verse 19).

These are the qualities which Christ longs to see among his people. And this is the kind of church which people will be attracted to. Not a church obsessed with its own survival, not a church treated as a club by its members, not a church more concerned with keeping its doctrine clean than with getting its hands dirty. But a church whose members are committed to each other and to their Lord and who overflow with costly love to their neighbours.

A church building in Holland has a stained glass window depicting faith, hope and love. From the inside you see them in that order. But from the outside the order is reversed. People must be able to see love in action if they are to discover hope and be drawn to faith in Christ.

Jezebel

Despite these qualities, all is not well at Thyatira. 'Nevertheless, I have this against you. You tolerate that woman Jezebel, who calls herself a prophetess. By her teaching she misleads my servants into sexual immorality and the eating of food sacrificed to idols' (verse 20). Let us try to reconstruct the situation.

There is in the church a woman of great spiritual power, who has gained quite a following by her forceful teaching, her commanding personality, and her 'words from the Lord' which seem so relevant, so persuasive. And what is her message that has caught so many people's imaginations? She teaches that full involvement in the trade-guilds is what the Lord expects of his people. He has set them free from all the scruples that might hold them back from attendance at the trade-guild dinners and the temple rituals. He calls them even to explore 'the deep things of Satan' (verse 24) – to immerse themselves in pagan society in the sure knowledge that their relationship with God cannot be harmed by such pursuits.

'Christians who keep themselves apart from the world', she says, 'are timid, pathetic creatures who know nothing of the freedom of the Spirit.' And what could be more reassuring for a Christian baker or dyer in Thyatira than to hear from her 'on the authority of the Holy Spirit' that it is wrong to separate from the world of business?

To those who admire this woman and embrace her teaching John's message comes as a shock: 'You tolerate that woman Jezebel' (verse 20).

'Jezebel' is John's name for her. No name expresses more chillingly the corruption of true religion by compromise with the worship of false gods. What the Nicolaitans stood for in Pergamum, this woman embodies in Thyatira.

The original Jezebel was a Phoenician princess whom King Ahab of Israel married to seal a political alliance. She brought with her to Ahab's palace not only her own worship of the fertility god Baal, but a staff of 450 prophets of Baal, 400 prophets of his consort Asherah, a domineering personality and a crusading zeal to seduce Israel from the worship of God to that of Baal. God met that threat by sending Elijah to stand up to her and to challenge the people. In the famous episode on Mount Carmel, Elijah demanded to know: 'How long will you waver between two opinions? If the Lord is God, follow him; but if Baal is God, then follow him' (1 Kings 18:21).

Now John plays Elijah to this woman's Jezebel. He demands that the church abandon all compromise between Christ and the expectations of pagan society. Christians may give to Caesar what is Caesar's, but they must not give him the worship due to God alone. To dabble with the emperor-cult may be 'what everybody does' in Thyatira if they want to get on in business, but for Christians it is a kind of 'sexual immorality' (verse 20). Like Hosea and Jeremiah before him, John finds in sexual unfaithfulness a telling picture of religious compromise.

In our own day, perhaps, we are inclined to have sympathy with 'Jezebel's' followers. We value tolerance and flexibility more than rigid principles and zealous purity. What could be more reasonable than the suggestion that unless we are immersed in the world's everyday affairs we are in no position to offer a Christian witness to society? Are we not supposed to be 'salt' and 'light' in the world? Yet John is telling us that there are times when the only authentic

witness to Christ is the witness which accepts the risk of
being misunderstood and isolated from society for the sake
of loyalty to the true God. It is the silent witness of suffering
and death, like the witness of Christ himself.

Those of us who are temperamentally compromisers
rather than defiant confronters of social evil and false religion are wise to ask ourselves occasionally: Can I imagine a
situation in which I would *have* to take a stand, whatever the
cost, against something which seemed seriously at odds
with my Christian faith. Or would I always find a way of
fudging the issue?

Put yourself in the position of these Christians at Thyatira.
Would you be attracted to 'Jezebel's' progressive message? Or
would you see John's point that it is all leading to the extinction of genuine, Christ-centred faith? Or imagine yourself a
member of King Ahab's court when Elijah turns up to
denounce the king for allowing himself to be seduced by the
false gods brought along by his wife. Do you dismiss Elijah
as a religious crank who doesn't understand how the world's
affairs have to be conducted these days? Or are you glad that
at least in him there shines a light to pierce the darkness?

True and false prophecy

John's confrontation with 'Jezebel' raises sharply the question of how we distinguish between the true and the false
prophet. Churches today which are open to the renewal of
the Holy Spirit and eager to experience spiritual gifts have
to face this difficulty.

Sometimes dangerous teaching comes with the attractive certainty of prophetic utterance. A respected Christian leader declares that in a vision the Lord has revealed to him that the final coming of Christ will occur before a certain date. A visitor to a loyal but struggling church reveals to them that their ineffectiveness is a judgment on their sheer lack of faith, and leads them to think that more admissions of guilt and more agonized heart-searching will at last lead to a change of fortune. Or in a period of worship someone assures a congregation, with 'a word from the Lord', that all is well with them and they have nothing to be concerned about or to repent of.

How can we know that such messages may not be from the Lord himself, but may be simply expressions of the speakers' hopes or hang-ups? After all, John too is speaking as a prophet, claiming to express what the risen Lord says to the churches. How do we know that his word is genuine and other messages may not be genuine? The answer will often not be clear-cut. Perhaps it was not immediately obvious even to the first readers of John's Revelation, for the book was not automatically part of Scripture. It became part of Scripture because the churches which first received it, and other Christians who came to use it over the next couple of centuries, agreed that it spoke to them with the authentic voice of Christ, and nurtured their life in the face of suffering.

The Bible itself proposes a number of tests for discerning whether prophecy is genuine, since from the beginning of their history the people of God have had to learn to distinguish between true and false prophets. The New Testament includes the following tests:

- 'Does the content of a prophecy and the character of the prophet conform to the teaching of Christ and his apostles (Mt. 7:20–23; 1 Jn. 4:6)?

- Does the message bring honour to Christ (Jn. 16:14)?

- Does it build up the church (1 Cor. 14:3–4)?

- Is it delivered with love (1 Cor. 13)?

- Does the rest of the church, and particularly its mature leaders, sense that God is indeed speaking through the prophet's word (1 Cor. 14:29)?

We need to assess carefully every insight for which special divine origin is claimed. It is not the impressiveness of the speaker, but the conformity of the message to these guidelines, which matters.

Modern trade-guilds

Trade-guilds made valuable contributions to society. They adorned the city centre by putting up statues to notable citizens. They provided occasional dinners for the poor of the town. But such good works are not, in John's eyes, an adequate reason for approving them and staying in them. The religious compromise involved in membership outweighs their positive value.

This is not to say, of course, that Christians today should withdraw from social and business associations with people

who do not share their faith. As Paul wrote to the church at
Corinth, if we were to avoid people who worship idols we
'would have to withdraw from society altogether' (1 Cor.
5:9-10). We need *more* Christians, not fewer, who will play
their part in trade unions, rotary clubs, townswomen's
guilds, political parties and football teams.

But some groups in society express in their official documents beliefs about God which are less than Christian.
Others involve their members in practices in which a
Christian could not happily take part. We have to make
judgments about where to draw the line between positive
engagement with society and unacceptable compromise of
Christian beliefs and values.

Warning and promise

'Jezebel' has been warned before: 'I have given her time to
repent of her immorality, but she is unwilling' (verse 21).
Now judgment is on its way. She fancies the bed on which
guests would recline with her at the dinners for which she
enthuses. But she will get the bed of suffering. And so will
her followers if they do not change their ways. 'I will make
those who commit adultery with her suffer intensely, unless
they repent of their ways. I will strike her children dead'
(verses 22-23).

As punishment for their 'adultery' with false religion
these followers of Jezebel are threatened with suffering and
even death – unless they repent. There is to be no doubt that
'I am he who searches hearts and minds, and I will repay

each of you according to your deeds' (verse 23). This does not, however, imply that all Christians who compromise their faith like the followers of 'Jezebel' will suffer illness or death as a consequence. Often God's judgment on wrong-doers consists in his allowing them through their actions to drift away from a real relationship with him. When he does that he is respecting the freedom which he himself in his love has given them.

Such language about God's judgment sounds harsh to us who have become uncomfortable with any talk about God which makes him sound intolerant of opposition or unsym-pathetic to human frailty. But we must recognize that the idea of judgment actually safeguards something which is vital to our understanding of what it is to be human: our sense of responsibility. The prospect of being judged by God means that we are accountable to him – that he takes us seriously, and what we do *matters* to him. If there were no judgment, *nothing* would matter in the long run, and we would be less than human.

But there is a brighter side, a promise to those who hold firm against Jezebel's insidious teaching: 'I will give author-ity over the nations – "He will rule them with an iron sceptre; he will dash them to pieces like pottery" – just as I have received authority from my Father. I will also give him the morning star' (verses 26–28).

This sounds at first like a promise that God's faithful people will one day be able to get their own back on those who have oppressed them. But no. Quoting a Psalm about the Messiah (Ps. 2:6–7), it promises that they will conquer the world by the same means as the Messiah himself has conquered – through their suffering and death. John's message is not a promise that they will get their own back, but a call to mission. Pagan resistance and oppression will be smashed, not by meeting force with force, but by the love which accepts suffering and experiences the transforming power of God in the midst of human powerlessness.

The 'morning star' alludes to the prophecy of Balaam in Numbers 24:17 – 'a star will come out of Jacob, a sceptre will rise out of Israel' – which came to be understood as a promise of the Messiah. Jesus himself is called 'the bright Morning Star' in Revelation 22:16.

But for readers in the Roman empire it had another significance too. The morning star was the planet Venus. In the ancient world the goddess Venus was a symbol of authority, especially for the Caesars, who claimed to be descended from her. In AD 95 – probably very close to the time when Revelation was written – a Roman poet anxious to flatter the emperor Domitian compared him to the morning star. So the final word to the church at Thyatira is an encouragement to mission in the knowledge that Christ, not Caesar, is the one who really holds authority over the nations. Christ, not Caesar, offers hope which grows brighter day by day.

Questions for reflection and discussion

1. What particularly in this chapter has helped you or made you think?

2. Re-read the paragraph beginning, 'These are the qualities which Christ longs to see among his people...' (page 75). What would you add, both positively and negatively, to the characteristics suggested there?

3. 'I am he who searches hearts and minds, and I will repay each of you according to your deeds' (Rev. 2:23). How can we help Christians to see this note of responsibility as something to be welcomed rather than feared or rejected?

4. How can the church encourage its members to develop and use their gifts without allowing powerful personalities such as 'Jezebel' to dominate and mislead people?

To the angel of the church in Sardis write: These are the words of him who holds the seven spirits of God and the seven stars. I know your deeds; you have a reputation of being alive, but you are dead. Wake up! Strengthen what remains and is about to die, for I have not found your deeds complete in the sight of my God. Remember, therefore, what you have received and heard; obey it, and repent. But if you do not wake up, I will come like a thief, and you will not know at what time I will come to you.

Yet you have a few people in Sardis who have not soiled their clothes. They will walk with me, dressed in white, for they are worthy. He who overcomes will, like them, be dressed in white. I will never blot out his name from the book of life, but will acknowledge his name before my Father and his angels. He who has an ear, let him hear what the Spirit says to the churches.

Revelation 3:1–6

CHAPTER 6

The Church at Sardis – harmless and ineffective

(Revelation 3:1-6)

Thirty-five miles south of Thyatira the road from the north meets the route which connects Smyrna with eastern Asia Minor, and eventually with Mesopotamia and Persia. Commanding the crossroads was Sardis, a city famous to the Greeks in history and legend as capital of the ancient kingdom of Lydia.

Here in the sixth century ruled Croesus, reputedly the richest man in the world. It was also here, in 546 BC, that he lost his kingdom to Cyrus the Persian. 450 metres above the Hermus valley, the acropolis of Sardis rises like a gigantic watchtower, its summit surrounded almost completely by precipices. Convinced the fortress was impregnable, Croesus' soldiers offered no resistance when Cyrus' men scaled the cliff-face under cover of darkness. So Sardis was captured, and the story became in Greek folklore the classic example of pride before a fall, misplaced trust in riches, and lack of watchfulness. But even the familiarity of the story did not prevent Sardis from falling once more, in

214 BC, through the negligence of its defenders, to Antiochus III of Syria.

Under Roman power the city continued to flourish commercially. Yet, prosperous though it was, Sardis was a city living on its past reputation. The heady days of Croesus lived on in the folk memory, but could not be recaptured.

The church asleep

In the earlier letters, Christ has given the good news before bringing the bad news to which the church must face up. But the church at Sardis gets no such gentle build-up. Jesus has no more severe message than this one. First he reminds them who he is. 'These are the words of him who holds the seven spirits of God and the seven stars' (verse 1). 'The seven spirits' is John's unusual way of describing the Holy Spirit (compare Rev. 1:4; 4:5; 5:6). Christ gives his Spirit to bring life and energy to his people, and only the Spirit can meet the church's desperate need. He also holds the seven stars – the churches themselves. For all their feebleness he has not let them go, and that is where their hope lies.

But there can be no hope unless there is a facing up to reality, and for the moment the church at Sardis is living under a dangerous delusion. 'I know your deeds; you have a reputation of being alive, but you are dead' (verse 1). Like the city in which it is set, the church has a reputation from the past. But there is no corresponding reality in the present. And no one has noticed. The church itself has not noticed, because it is asleep. That is why it is urged to 'wake up' (verse 2).

People outside the church have not noticed either. 'You have a reputation of being alive.' Listen to what they are saying: 'That church has been the mainstay of our village life. I couldn't bear to see it close.' 'They run a jolly good scout troop.' 'The vicar is so nice when he visits you in hospital.'

The church at Sardis is a church of which everybody speaks well. Everybody, that is, except Christ himself. What is his complaint? The church, quite bluntly, is dead. That is not obvious outwardly. It is not a dwindling congregation of elderly people. It has not been brought to the verge of extinction by the ravages of persecution or heresy. It is serenely unaware that the peace which it enjoys is the peace of the cemetery. It is the perfect model of inoffensive Christianity.

Of course, for a church to enjoy a harmonious relationship with the community which surrounds it is not wrong in itself. Jesus pronounced a blessing on peace-makers (Mt. 5:9). And Paul urged the Christians at Rome: 'If it is possible, as far as it depends on you, live at peace with everyone' (Rom. 12:18). But his words clearly imply that there will be some circumstances where peace is not possible.

When a church takes a stand against prevailing attitudes and practices in society, it will lose popularity. When it insists that Christ is not just one possible saviour among many but is Lord of the universe, it will provoke hostility. When its members actually make the Sermon on the Mount (Mt. 5-7) their very life-blood, they will make people feel that the rules by which the world operates are being undermined.

Erich Honecker, President of Communist East Germany, was deposed in 1989's autumn of peaceful

revolution. Thrown out of his official residence, he was welcomed and cared for in the home of a Lutheran pastor who
understood Jesus' words, 'Love your enemies and pray for
those who persecute you' (Mt. 5:44). The pastor was bitterly criticized for 'harbouring a criminal', and some
abandoned the church because of it.

When the gospel is preached *and lived*, people cannot for
ever be indifferent. But the church at Sardis has avoided
such discomfort. Like a chameleon, it has simply melted
into its surroundings and become indistinguishable from
them. It has become outstandingly successful at the art of
camouflage.

A church in danger of death

The church at Sardis was on the verge of death. A church
today is in danger of death when its members:

● Bask in its past reputation rather than being open to
God's leading now;

● are more concerned about rules and traditions than about
love or Jesus;

● cease to believe that a creative God may have new things
to teach them, new tasks for them to do, new directions
for them to take;

● regard their church as a club for like-minded people
rather than as God's people called 'to declare the

wonderful deeds of him who called you out of darkness into his marvellous light' (1 Pet. 2:9, RSV);

● have not learnt that there can be no discipleship where there is no denying self, taking up the cross, and following in the footsteps of Jesus (Mk. 8:34);

● are more concerned that their church should project a positive image than that it should reflect the character of Jesus;

● are so busy with church activities that they have no time to get close to their neighbours or to be involved in service to the local community;

● value 'decency and order' in worship more highly than the disturbance of the Holy Spirit;

● dampen the enthusiasm of their young people by assuring themselves that 'they will grow out of it';

● regard their church as an unchanging haven of security in a constantly changing world, rather than as a base from which to respond to the challenges of the world;

Wake up!

Yet there remains the possibility of revival. Like the city which twice fell victim to invading armies because it failed to be watchful, the church is called to wake up, to keep alert, before the rest of its life finally drains away. Then comes a sad and devastating comment on the church's performance. 'I have not found your deeds complete in the sight of my God' (verse 2). They are so lacking in commitment and perseverance that no service they undertake ever gets finished. Their works may pass human scrutiny, but that is a different matter from examination 'in the sight of my God'.

What he longs to see is an overflowing of 'love and faith, service and perseverance' (Rev. 2:19). In a modern world where television has reduced people's attention span to about three minutes, and there are so many alternative activities to distract us from the task in hand, endurance is in scarce supply.

If the moribund church is to be restored to life, it must shake itself out of its slumbers. How can we do this? It means obedience to three commands. 'Remember, therefore, what you have received and heard; obey it, and repent' (verse 3).

First, *remember*. Memory is a powerful aid to making a fresh start. In particular, we need to remember the message of God's love for us and the guidelines about Christian living which we received when we first found life in Christ. It is so easy to drift away from joyful obedience to Christ into a comfortable acceptance of mediocrity. As in a human love-relationship, we must allow the first feelings of extravagant emotion to mature into a steady self-giving to the one who has captured our love. And for that we need to keep reflecting on the teaching which will feed us and guide us on the Christian way.

Second, *obey*. This is an important word in John's Revelation, written as it is for people under constant pressure to escape from danger by abandoning the observance of Christ's demands. The same Greek word is there at the beginning of the book: 'Blessed are those who hear (the words of this prophecy) and *take to heart* what is written in it' (1:3). It is there at the end: 'Blessed is he who *keeps* the words of the prophecy in this book' (22:7).

The idea of obedience is not a popular one today. It sounds restrictive, even oppressive. It runs counter to our longing for freedom and personal expression. Yet the constant theme of Jesus' preaching is that real liberation is to be found not in casting off all restraint and 'doing our own thing', but only in surrender to the will of the one who made us. 'Whoever wants to save his life will lose it, but whoever loses his life for me and for the gospel will save it' (Mk. 8:35).

In the situation faced by John's churches the main focus of obedience is simply on remaining loyal to Jesus in face of pressure to deny him. As we shall see later, the church at Philadelphia is praised because 'you have kept my word and have not denied my name' (Rev. 3:8). In what ways do we deny his name? Probably not by publicly disowning him through fear of persecution, but in a thousand compromises such as those suggested on pages 90-1 where we described 'a church in danger of death'. So obedience for a church today will mean reflecting seriously on the questions raised there, and seeking to put things right.

We are unlikely to disobey Jesus by publicly disowning him. Yet our responses of obedience or disobedience to the thousand small challenges that come to us in everyday life are in fact building us into people who are able, or unable, to face the ultimate test.

And we never know when that stark challenge to acknowledge Christ or to deny him may come our way. In the spring of 1988 a plane was hijacked by Islamic extremists and flown to Cyprus. As it stood there on the tarmac the hijackers agreed eventually to allow Muslims among the hostages to go free. Twelve people were called forward to leave the plane. As they filed through the door the gunman counting them out noticed a cross tattooed on the wrist of one of them. 'What is that?' he asked. 'Aren't you a Muslim?' Imagine what thoughts raced through the man's mind in that second before he replied, 'No, I'm a Christian, a Coptic Christian from Egypt.' Even so, he was allowed to continue his walk to freedom.

The third command is to *repent*. The church needs consciously and deliberately to renounce its drift into death, to turn back to Christ. Otherwise he will come to them in judgment. Just as invaders came by night to a casual and careless Sardis, 'I will come like a thief, and you will not know at what time I will come to you' (verse 3).

Jesus used the imagery of the thief to refer to his final coming at the end of all things (Mt. 24:42–51), but here the warning implies a coming of Christ within history. The Christ who will finally come to bring judgment and salvation is constantly coming, to bless and to judge, in the events of history and in the experience of his people. What form the coming to Sardis will take is not explained. But perhaps Christ is warning, as he warned the church at Ephesus (2:5), that their very existence as a church is under threat.

A faithful few

Now for the good news. Even in Sardis Christ finds a few who have resisted the pressure to drift away from their distinctive Christian life-style. These 'have not soiled their clothes' (verse 4). They have not become identified with the mediocre moral standards of their surroundings.

The citizens of Sardis in fact had a reputation for bad character and constant feuds between its citizens. The pagan philosopher Apollonius, a contemporary of John, wrote letters addressed to the people of Sardis, with messages such as:

> *There are no prizes among you for good character, for what good character do you have? But if you competed for the first prize in vice, you would all win it at once... Why have you engaged in this endless war among yourselves — a war between children, young men, grown men, old men, and even women and girls?... It is right that an old-fashioned philosopher like me should wish to visit a city so ancient and famous as yours. And I would willingly have visited it without waiting for an invitation, if I had any hopes of bringing your city into harmony with morality, with nature, with law or with God.*

If that is how bad things were, it is all the more shocking that the church in Sardis could not easily be distinguished from the surrounding culture. But a few have kept fresh their love for the Lord and have maintained their distinctive lifestyle. To encourage them there are three promises.

Three promises

First, a promise of victory. 'They will walk with me, dressed in white, for they are worthy. He who overcomes will, like them, be dressed in white' (verses 4–5). Roman citizens wore a pure white toga at a triumphal celebration, when they lined the streets of Rome to welcome a victorious general and his troops on their return from the battlefield. The point would not be lost on readers in Sardis – notoriously a city of defeat and no longer the scene of royal triumphs. Most of the church is unprepared for the coming of Christ its King. But when he comes the expectant few will walk with him in his triumphal procession.

The second promise is about the 'book of life'. 'I will never erase his name from the book of life' (verse 5). Greek cities kept registers of their citizens, from which the names of those who proved unworthy were sometimes removed. Jews thought of God keeping a book in which the names of all his people were inscribed as a sign of their security in him (Ex. 32:32; Ps. 69:28; Dan. 12:1–2).

But there is probably here another layer of meaning too. Synagogue worship included a prayer for the destruction of those who turned against Jewish belief and practice: 'May they be blotted out of the book of life and not enrolled among the righteous'. Increasing tension between Jews and Christians after AD 70 meant that Christians began to be included among the heretics against whom this curse was directed. Christians – even Jewish Christians – began to feel less welcome in the synagogues. Maybe in some places their names were removed from the synagogue-register.

Deprived of the synagogue's protection, they were exposed to the risk of persecution by the city authorities.

But here Christ assures them of their place in the book of life. Whatever their enemies may threaten, the One who really has power over their destiny guarantees their absolute security.

Thirdly, a promise of acknowledgment before God. 'I will acknowledge his name before my Father and his angels' (verse 5). Here the risen Christ echoes words of the earthly Jesus in Matthew 10:32: 'Whoever acknowledges me before others, I will also acknowledge before my Father in heaven'. It is all a question of 'confessing the name' of Jesus. If most of the church at Sardis have kept quiet about Jesus for fear of the consequences, there remain the few who have readily confessed that they belong to him. And those who acknowledge in the presence of others that they belong to him may be sure that he will acknowledge in God's presence that they are his.

Is it right to leave a church?

The faithful handful in Sardis must have asked themselves, as we would, 'How long can we stay in this dead set-up? We seem to be unable to influence the others. Should we not withdraw from them and start a new church, meeting in one of our homes?' The option of leaving their church and joining another one down the road was not of course open to them, as it is to many of us, since there was no other church down the road or even in another part of town. But they could in principle have washed their hands of the rest of the church and made a fresh start in a different meeting-place.

But they did not. It is significant that, despite all the problems in the seven churches, there is no suggestion in Revelation that faithful Christians should withdraw from corrupt congregations and form a new church somewhere else. Instead there is the repeated emphasis that Christ holds the churches in his hand, that he calls his people to repentance and holds out the promise of restoration.

In our very different circumstances, we should perhaps not rule out the possibility of moving from a church for the sake of our own – or our children's – spiritual health, or because our church is having a negative impact in the neighbourhood, or indeed because we have gifts to offer to another church which are already present in abundance in our present church. But we should never make a move without careful thought and prayer. Such mobility is a luxury which is not really open to Christians like those at Sardis for whom the possibility of oppression lies not far round the corner. Certainly the weight of New Testament evidence is on the side of staying where you are and drawing on God's strength to be faithful there. A survivor's guide to such a situation would include the following advice:

● Ensure that those who share your vision for a lively church keep the vision alive through informal contacts for prayer and encouragement.

- But do not become a clique separated from the rest of the church – you will not win them over unless you stick with them!

- Keep your own Christian life healthy through the stimulus of links with Christians elsewhere, for example in ecumenical groups, and through teaching received at conferences or from books or tapes.

- Communicate your vision gently but clearly with as many in the church as you can. Don't assume that everyone is against you. There are always some who lack vitality not because they are hostile to spiritual values but because they are confused through inadequate teaching.

- If you are one of the church's leaders, try to get other leaders to agree on some plans for teaching and action designed to develop full-blooded discipleship.

- If you are not a leader, prayerfully consider how the church's leaders may be helped to take responsibility for change. Tell them, perhaps, that there is a desire for a Bible study and prayer group and ask them to help you start it.

- Learn from John's Revelation that there is risk and pain in playing the prophetic role, but learn also that Christ has power to change people and he hasn't given up on your church.

● Take heart from the experience of Sardis. The church must have taken some notice of John's message, for we know that it remained alive in the second century, and produced a remarkable leader named Melito. He was a man with prophetic gifts, and was the first Christian we know of to make a pilgrimage to the Holy Land. His writings include a notable sermon on the Passover, and a petition to the emperor Marcus Aurelius arguing that there is no good reason why the state should prosecute people simply for being Christians.

● If in the end you believe you must leave your church, do it in a positive way. Explain to the leaders your reasons, and find a new church where your contribution can benefit others.

Questions for reflection and discussion

1. What particularly in this chapter has helped you or made you think?

2. Imagine you are an outsider looking at your church noticeboards. What impression would you get of the church's priorities and of what makes its members 'tick'? On reflection, do you want to suggest any changes to the noticeboards?

3. How do you react to the story about Erich Honecker on page 90-1. Can you think of any parallel situations in your own experience?

4. Look at the section headed 'A church in danger of death'. What are the most serious dangers for your church at the moment? What might be done to change things?

To the angel of the church in Philadelphia write: These are the words of him who is holy and true, who holds the key of David. What he opens no-one can shut, and what he shuts no-one can open. I know your deeds. See, I have placed before you an open door that no-one can shut. I know that you have little strength, yet you have kept my word and have not denied my name. I will make those who are of the synagogue of Satan, who claim to be Jews though they are not, but are liars — I will make them come and fall down at your feet and acknowledge that I have loved you. Since you have kept my command to endure patiently, I will also keep you from the hour of trial that is going to come upon the whole world to test those who live on the earth.

I am coming soon. Hold on to what you have, so that no-one will take your crown. Him who overcomes I will make a pillar in the temple of my God. Never again will he leave it. I will write on him the name of my God and the name of the city of my God, the new Jerusalem, which is coming down out of heaven from my God; and I will also write on him my new name. He who has an ear, let him hear what the Spirit says to the churches.

Revelation 3:7–13

CHAPTER 7

The Church at Philadelphia – ready for mission

(Revelation 3:7-13)

The very name of Philadelphia – 'brotherly love' – recalls that characteristically Christian quality which New Testament writers constantly urged upon their churches. The name in fact commemorates the proverbial loyalty to each other of two rulers of Pergamum, the brothers Attalus and Eumenes, one of whom founded the city in the second century BC. Several features of the city help us to understand the message of the risen Christ to its church.

First, the reason for its foundation is significant. The site of Philadelphia lay where the borders of the three ancient countries of Mysia, Lydia and Phrygia met. The city was planted as a base from which the Greek language and civilization could be spread to the barbarian tribes of Phrygia. It was a city with a mission. Situated on the main road thirty miles south-east of Sardis, it was ideally located to pursue its missionary task.

Secondly, the city lived in constant fear of earthquakes. It suffered from a great earthquake in AD 17 and continued to experience smaller tremors for months or even years afterwards. Strabo, who visited it shortly after the earthquake, said Philadelphia was

> ...*full of earthquakes, for the walls never cease being cracked, and different parts of the city are constantly suffering damage. That is why the actual town has few inhabitants, but the majority live as farmers in the countryside, as they have fertile land. But one is surprised even at the few, that they are so fond of the place when they have such insecure dwellings.*

So the people of Philadelphia lived always under the shadow of disaster. And many of them chose to live outdoors, away from the city's buildings.

Thirdly, the city took on a new name after the emperor Tiberius had helped to get it back on its feet following the earthquake of AD 17. It became known as Neocaesarea – 'new city of Caesar', or 'city of the young Caesar'. It reverted to its old name after two or three decades. But when Flavius Vespasian was emperor, about twenty years before the writing of Revelation, it came to be called Philadelphia Flavia. So on two occasions in the recent past Philadelphia had taken a new name from the imperial 'god'.

Fourthly, the city suffered at the hands of Domitian. Now that he had become emperor, he upset this sense of gratitude for imperial aid. In AD 92 he issued a decree requiring at least half the vineyards in the provinces to be cut down and no new ones planted – an act bitterly unpopular in the province of Asia. Domitian's intention was probably to stimulate corn production. Philadelphia's soil, rich in lava sediments from extinct volcanoes, produced vines in abundance, but was not so suitable for corn.

So Domitian's decree must have seemed to its citizens like the action of an enemy, and a particularly cynical enemy at that. For even in times of war it was an unwritten law in their part of the world not to damage the enemy's vines or olive trees, since both require years to mature. We shall see as we go along how these four aspects of the city's experience are drawn on in the letter.

Christ, holy and true

In contrast to the fickleness of imperial patronage, Christ announces himself as the one 'who is holy and true, who holds the key of David. What he opens no-one can shut, and what he shuts, no-one can open' (verse 7). There are a number of themes running here. 'Holy One' is a Jewish title for the Messiah (see John 6:69). So the risen Christ is asserting that he is the real Messiah, despite the objections of Philadelphia's hostile Jews, 'the synagogue of Satan' (verse 9). Though they may deny it, *he* is the one who has 'David's key', he is the one who has power to welcome people into God's presence or to exclude them from it.

The mention of 'David's key' alludes to Isaiah 22:22, where Eliakim, the faithful steward of king Hezekiah, holds the key by which he controls entry to the king's house. So here is a promise to Jewish Christians in Philadelphia experiencing exclusion from the synagogue: the Jewish authorities may close the synagogue door on you, but

Christ welcomes you into the presence of the King. Despite Jewish resistance, Christ has opened the door for Gentiles to join the people of God.

But the promise is at the same time a challenge. The open door offers a vision of men and women streaming in as Christ himself calls them to be his people. It is a vision which he expects the church in Philadelphia to share, for he has confidence in their faithfulness. 'You have kept my word and have not denied my name... You have kept my command to endure patiently' (verses 8, 10). Christ can pay no greater compliment to a church than to describe it as reflecting his own character. Just as he is 'the True One' (verse 7) – the one who keeps his word – so the Christians at Philadelphia have kept his word under stress.

The open door

This is no whizz-kid church with computerized mailing lists, five paid staff and its own rock band. 'I know that you have little strength' (verse 8). It is a comparatively weak church in a city which has had the stuffing knocked out of it by Domitian's decree about the vines. And yet the door which means security for them can become the door of opportunity for mission to others.

This way of talking about mission is well known from Paul's letters. 'I will stay on at Ephesus until Pentecost,' he writes, 'because a great door for effective work has opened to me, and there are many who oppose me' (1 Cor.16:8-9). And he urges the Christians at Colossae to pray for him and for Timothy, 'that God may open a door for our message' (Col. 4:3; see also 2 Cor. 2:12).

And the image would be especially vivid for Christians in Philadelphia, whose own city had been founded for a 'missionary' purpose, to spread Greek culture to uncivilized tribespeople. Now the same lines of communication which had made that possible are available for the church to declare the good news of Jesus to the surrounding region. Christ himself has put his people there to carry out his purpose, and he takes responsibility for the outcome of their missionary efforts. 'I have placed before you an open door that no-one can shut' (verse 8).

Are Jewish people among those who will benefit from this mission of the church at Philadelphia, or are they to be written off for ever as 'the synagogue of Satan, who claim to be Jews though they are not'(verse 9)? By shutting the door on Christians who sought the protection of the synagogue from inquisition by the state, have the Jews closed the door on their own entry into God's kingdom? What is the meaning of the promise, 'I will make them come and fall down at your feet and acknowledge that I have loved you' (verse 9)? Does John hope to see non-Christian Jews grovelling at the church's feet and admitting – too late for their own salvation – that they were wrong?

No. John is turning upside down passages in Isaiah which foretell the acceptance of Gentiles by Israel's God (Is. 45:14; 49:6). But now it is not the Gentile oppressors of Israel who must learn to recognize Israel's special place in God's purpose. It is the Jewish persecutors of the church who must come to see that the church, Jewish and Gentile, is the special object of God's love. John's confidence in this possibility rests on his confidence in Christ's power. It is because he has opened a door which no one else can shut that the church's witness can bring antagonistic Jews into an experience of Christ's love.

Perhaps at this point we should recall what was said earlier about the relations between John's churches and the Jewish people. The first readers of John's Revelation were experiencing a good deal of hostility from Jewish neighbours and were struggling with how to react to it. Other parts of the New Testament and other documents of the period demonstrate that such tensions between church and synagogue were a feature of the times. For those Christians to label the Jewish community as 'the synagogue of Satan' is to use language which makes us uncomfortable. But it is not anti-Semitism. It is an understandable expression of the exasperation felt by those – both Jew and Gentile – who had discovered in Jesus their Messiah and wished that the people of the synagogue shared this discovery. It gives no reason for modern followers of the Jew Jesus to express hostility towards today's Jews.

The open door and the church's mission

If it is Christ who opens doors through which the church may go to share the good news, we need to learn how to recognize an open door when it lies before us, and how to seize the opportunity which it presents. What might this involve?

- Be encouraged by the fact that Christ himself takes responsibility for opening the door. What he opens, no one can shut. It is his Spirit's work to create in people a hunger for God and to open their eyes to his truth. This will preserve us from frantic efforts to prise open doors which may be shut tight at the moment, and enable us to trust him to lead us to people who are responsive.

- Be like the church at Philadelphia! Don't wait until you are strong before being adventurous in mission, or you may wait for ever. Count on Christ's power to use you more than on your own readiness to take on the world!

- Be ready to realize that there may be more doors open than you have previously dreamt possible. Since we know that Christ longs for all people to discover God's love through him, it would not be surprising if more people were ready to take the Christian message seriously than we ever dared to imagine. When I met someone who had become a Christian in his thirties he asked, almost angrily, 'Why did no one tell me this great news before?'

- Recognize that many people's apparent indifference to the church arises because they do not *perceive* that we have anything relevant or life-changing to share with them. There may be many reasons for this, but two in particular stand out.

- Perhaps they cannot see a deep and challenging quality of life lived out in the Christian community – either because it isn't there, or because we live it so privately that they have no opportunity to notice!

● Or perhaps the language we use to express our faith rings no bells with them. It doesn't seem to touch their own concerns. We seem to them to be operating in a mysterious private world of religion which doesn't touch everyday life. We don't scratch where people itch. Christ himself understands inside out their concerns and their experience, as the letter to Philadelphia shows. He knows what the city as well as the church has gone through, and he expresses his message in a way which is in tune with that. He is a model for us. We learn to understand people by listening rather than by talking.

● Give priority to friendships. Only when we are involved with people in genuine, caring friendship will we learn what their real concerns are. And most people who are won to Christ are won through the influence of a friend.

● Don't work from the assumption that people are uninterested, hostile or totally blind to the gospel. Even in a very secular society, huge numbers of people are interested in spiritual values. This may show itself in concern about the environment, or in exploration of the New Age movement. It may surface in the sense of wonder at the birth of a baby. Such signs may not be evidence of a lively relationship with God, but they are signs of a search going on. We should see them as searchings to be built on rather than as inadequate ideas to be put down.

● Don't assume that people who have no obvious sense of need will not be interested in the gospel. The gospel is not a psychological crutch for inadequate people, it is good news of God's loving purpose for people of all kinds. For ordinary, well-adjusted human beings the starting-point may be the search for truth or the appropriateness of thankfulness to God for the good experiences of life. Yes, they do have need of forgiveness for wrongdoing and for being out of step with God, but they may not realize that until they have begun to be attracted by another aspect of the Christian message.

● Recognize your unique opportunities. No one else has *your* network of friends, *your* places of influence. Ho Chi Minh, father of communist Vietnam, was at one time a dish-washer in the Carlton Hotel, Pall Mall. What if a Christian had been there alongside him?

● Don't waste too much time lamenting the doors that are closed, but make the most of the open doors. Readers of this book who visit the seven churches may be aware of the enormous obstacles to evangelism in Turkey today. But there are 1,500,000 Turkish 'guest-workers' in western Europe. In these new surroundings many of them are able to hear the gospel in a new way, and the fact that some are exploited as cheap labour is an opportunity for Christians to stand with them in the struggle for justice.

● Recognize that mission is the work of the church, not simply of individuals. The door is open to the church community, not simply to enthusiastic individuals. The consistent life of a Christian community has great power to persuade. And, if we are to keep going, we all need the complementary gifts and the encouragement of each other.

● Recognize that Christ's mission, however fruitful it may be, will always meet with some resistance. Then is the time to remember again that the outcome is Christ's own responsibility, and to trust in him who says, '*I have placed before you an open door that no-one can shut.*'

The rewards of faithfulness

Christ makes rich promises to the church which serves him faithfully.

Honoured by God. 'Since you have kept my command to endure patiently, I will also keep you...' (verse 10). Christ always honours the unspectacular loyalty of his servants. The film *Chariots of Fire* tells how at the 1924 Olympic Games the Scottish athlete Eric Liddell declined to run in the heats of the hundred metres because they were held on a Sunday. He was entered instead for the four hundred metres, though he had little time to train adequately for the longer race. Just before the final he opened a note given to him earlier by the team's masseur. It quoted a text from 1 Samuel 2:30: 'He that honours me, I will honour'. Christian faithfulness for him had meant refusing to compete on Sunday, and now this text inspired him to run as he had never run before. He won the race, setting a new world record.

Preserved through suffering. John goes on to make the only reference in the seven letters to the ordeal with which the rest of Revelation is concerned. 'I will keep you from the hour of trial that is going to come upon the whole world to test those who live on the earth' (verse 10). This cannot mean that Christians are preserved from suffering, for the rest of Revelation warns of suffering and even martyrdom for them (Rev. 11:7-8; 6:9). It means that God will not abandon them in their time of trial. Samuel Rutherford, imprisoned for his faith in the seventeenth century, wrote: 'Jesus Christ came into my cell last night, and every stone flashed like a ruby.'

Brought into Christ's presence. 'I am coming soon' (verse 11). We have found mention of Christ's coming already in Revelation 2:5 and 3:3, where it referred not to his final coming but to a specific act of judgment on the church within the course of history. Here the promise is that Christ will soon act to demonstrate his care for the Philadelphian church. But every coming of Christ to his people, whether in judgment or blessing, is a foreshadowing of that final coming which will bring his people into the ultimate security of God's presence. The effects of that coming for Christ's faithful people are expressed in three images.

The *crown* or *garland* was the prize of victory in the athletic stadium. Christ urges, 'Hold on to what you have, so that no-one will take your crown' (verse 11).

The second image is that of the *pillar*. 'Him who overcomes I will make a pillar in the temple of my God' (verse 12). He will be built into the structure of the temple, and of course elsewhere in the New Testament the temple is a picture of the people of God filled with his presence (1 Cor. 3:9, 16–17). Whereas the citizens of Philadelphia were subject to constant uncertainty and often lived out in the open for fear of further earthquakes, the faithful Christian is permanently secure in God's temple: 'Never again will he leave it' (verse 12).

Thirdly, there is the image of the *name*. 'I will write on him the name of my God and the name of the city of my God, the new Jerusalem, which is coming down out of heaven from my God; and I will also write on him my new name' (verse 12). The name indicates God's ownership and protection (Rev. 7:3; 14:1; 22:4). Christians belong as citizens of the new Jerusalem, whose beauty contrasts sharply with the cracked buildings of earthquake-stricken Philadelphia. That city of God is where they will one day live, and from there they already derive strength and guidance for their lives.

They belong to Christ, whose new name is not disclosed because his future glory is to be even greater than the church has yet discovered. The reference to the new Jerusalem and Christ's new name recalls the new names which Philadelphia had – temporarily – taken in recent decades. But the new name of God's victorious people is no temporary change, no passing flattery of the latest 'god' in Rome. It is a sign of God's utter faithfulness and self-giving to those who trust themselves to his love.

Questions for reflection and discussion

1. What particularly in this chapter has helped you or made you think?

2. 'See, I have placed before you an open door that no-one can shut' (Rev. 3:8). What doors of opportunity for mission can you see in your own situation, and how can you take advantage of them?

3. 'I know you have little strength...' (Rev. 3:8). Do we sometimes let our sense of weakness stop us from acting adventurously in mission? How can God use our weaknesses?

4. Re-read the story about Eric Liddell on page 112. Can you think of occasions when you or someone whom you know has had a similar experience of faithfulness being honoured by God?

*T*o the angel of the church in Laodicea write: These are the words of the Amen, the faithful and true witness, the ruler of God's creation. I know your deeds, that you are neither cold nor hot. I wish you were either one or the other! So, because you are lukewarm — neither hot nor cold — I am about to spit you out of my mouth. You say, 'I am rich; I have acquired wealth and do not need a thing.' But you do not realise that you are wretched, pitiful, poor, blind and naked. I counsel you to buy from me gold refined in the fire, so that you can become rich; and white clothes to wear, so that you can cover your shameful nakedness; and salve to put on your eyes, so that you can see.

Those whom I love I rebuke and discipline. So be earnest, and repent. Here I am! I stand at the door and knock. If anyone hears my voice and opens the door, I will come in and eat with him, and he with me.

To him who overcomes, I will give the right to sit with me on my throne, just as I overcame and sat down with my Father on his throne. He who has an ear, let him hear what the Spirit says to the churches.

Revelation 3:14–22

CHAPTER 8

The Church at Laodicea – having everything, and nothing

(Revelation 3:14-22)

By the time he reaches Laodicea, John's messenger has travelled two hundred and fifty miles since leaving Ephesus, and he will cover a further hundred miles to complete the circle. Standing on a low hill on the southern side of the Lycus valley, Laodicea became prosperous because of its position at the junction of major routes. The main road actually passed through the centre of the city, entering through the Ephesian Gate on the western side and departing through the Syrian Gate on the eastern side.

Christ, the ruler of creation

Laodicea dominated the two other cities of the Lycus valley – Hierapolis, six miles north across the valley, and Colossae, ten miles to the east. Churches in all three cities are mentioned by Paul in Colossians 4:13. The church at Laodicea seems to have been influenced by the same false teaching as had developed in Colossae, which regarded Jesus as merely one of several intermediaries between God and human beings.

The description of Christ which opens this letter is the only one of the seven which does not allude directly to the vision of Revelation 1:12-20. There are other important things which the church at Laodicea needs to hear. He is 'the Amen, the faithful and true witness, the ruler of God's creation' (verse 14). 'The Amen' is a name of God himself in Isaiah 65:16 (translated 'the God of truth' in NIV). It means he is utterly reliable. He has all the firmness which, as we shall see, this church lacks. Christ has borne his witness in a way which perfectly portrays the truth about God's character and purpose.

'The ruler of God's creation', like the similar phrase in Colossians 1:15, shows that Christ is Lord over all that he has made, and infinitely superior to all other spiritual forces in the universe. This truth about Christ stands at the head of the letter, for it was the local tendency to soft-pedal his uniqueness which had sapped the church's sense of its calling.

The lukewarm church

'I know your deeds, that you are neither cold nor hot. I wish you were either one or the other! So, because you are luke-warm – neither hot nor cold – I am about to spit you out of my mouth' (verses 15–16). Speaking through John, the risen Christ here makes use of a well-known feature of the city's life to make his point. Laodicea's increasing prosperity had created an awkward problem. Its water supply was inadequate. Where was a reliable source to be found? The answer is indicated by the remains of an aqueduct which brought water from a supply south of Laodicea, perhaps from the hot mineral springs near Denizli, the modern town five miles away.

The aqueduct is unusual in that it is made of hollowed stone blocks, each about a cubic metre, laid in a double line along the ground. Water carried along the aqueduct would have remained warm. And deposits of calcium carbonate which remain on the stones show that the water cannot have been pleasant to drink. But it was all they could get, and they had to live with it.

Ancient writers make clear that hot water is for washing, and sometimes for medicinal use, while cold water is for drinking. Lukewarm water is good for neither purpose. How galling therefore it must have been for the prosperous citizens of Laodicea to know that the rival cities nearby could boast what they did not have. Across the valley they could see the sparkling white 'cliffs' of Hierapolis, formed by calcium carbonate deposits produced by water flowing out of hot springs. The medicinal powers of these springs were the basis of the city's reputation. And a few miles to the east Colossae had a supply of cold, pure spring water, wonderful to drink.

Each of Laodicea's neighbours, then, had water which was excellent for particular purposes. By contrast its own

water, though safe enough to drink, was more likely to provoke vomiting than to be drunk with pleasure. And that is
the point which Christ is driving home to the church. By
labelling them *lukewarm*, he is not – as is often supposed –
complaining about their lack of enthusiasm, or suggesting
that *hot* enthusiasm and *cold* resistance to him are both
preferable to half-heartedness. He is condemning 'your
deeds'. Just as the city, in contrast to its neighbours, has no
water which can supply life and health, so the church is
behaving in a way which serves no useful purpose. The
effect of their conduct on Christ is like the effect of the
city's water supply: it makes him sick.

The church which deceives itself

The nature of the church's conduct which provokes such
devastating condemnation is explained in verse 17: 'You say,
"I am rich; I have acquired wealth and do not need a thing."
But you do not realize that you are wretched, pitiful, poor,
blind and naked.' The trouble with the church at Laodicea
is that it has taken on the character of the city in which it
was placed. God's people have been squeezed into the
mould of the surrounding society. John's words here
skilfully play on three things of which the city was proud.
**First, Laodicea had long been a wealthy banking
centre**. When an earthquake in AD 60 destroyed much of
the city, its people rebuilt it from their own resources,
declining the usual financial help from Rome. Wealthy citizens endowed particular building programmes. One

financed the new stadium designed for gladiatorial contests. Another paid for the heating of covered walkways and piped oil for massaging at the public baths. They were well off, and pleased with their achievements. Yet in Christ's view the church in this city is poor.

Their second claim to fame was as a centre of medical excellence. Laodicea boasted a medical school. There was a strong tradition of ophthalmology in this area of Phrygia, and ancient medical writers speak about the healing properties of 'Phrygian stone'. This was apparently a powder made from various metallic salts, including the zinc compounds which are still used in eye ointments today. Galen, the second-century medical authority who came from Pergamum, wrote: 'You will strengthen the eyes by using the dry powder made of Phrygian stone, applying the mixture to the eyelids without touching the surface of the eye inside. For this is what women do every day, when they make their eyes glamorous.'

We may guess from such information and from what John writes in Revelation that Laodicea marketed extensively and profitably an ointment developed locally. Its exact composition was no doubt kept secret from commercial rivals. But the church in this city is 'blind'. Claiming to cure the blindness of others, it is blind to its own spiritual blindness.

Thirdly, the city was well known for its woollen products. Numerous garments were called 'Laodicean', as we might speak of an Aran sweater or a Cashmere jumper. And Laodicea had one special advantage over its rivals. It was famous for a breed of black sheep, which Strabo describes as follows:

*The country around Laodicea produces sheep remarkable not only for
the softness of their wool, in which they surpass even that of Miletus,
but also for its raven-black colour. And they get a splendid revenue
from it.*

Apparently Laodicea dispensed with the costs of dyeing for
the luxury market by promoting a fashion in black glossy
fabrics made from the natural fleeces of an animal
developed by its own breeders. You can almost see the
advertising slogan on packages of garments arriving in
Rome: 'Raven-black, the Style for the Nineties'.

But in this city of fine clothes, the church is 'naked'. In
proud and affluent Laodicea, the church is as self-satisfied as
its pagan neighbours. Thinking it has everything, it is in
reality 'wretched, pitiful, poor, blind and naked'. All the
banks, all the pharmacies, all the looms in the city cannot
provide for its needs.

The church in danger

When we read this letter we may be tempted to ask: Can a
church really become as bad as this? Surely it couldn't
happen to us? What actually makes a church 'poor, blind and
naked'? A little exploration may suggest to us that we are
exposed to dangers not entirely different from those experienced by the church at Laodicea.

The Laodiceans' smugness about their wealth has a
remarkably modern ring. Increasing prosperity has a numbing effect on Christians as on anyone else. We come to take

it for granted that our standard of living will continue to rise. We adjust our expenditure to take account of our pay increases. Even though we do not quite keep up with the Joneses, we prefer not to lag too far behind them. The whole clutter of materialism so easily blunts our spiritual awareness. We don't have to pray for our daily bread because we know it's waiting for us at Sainsbury's.

Gradually and unnoticed, the thought steals upon us that our everyday lives can continue without much attention to God. We can save him for the difficult times, when he'll be there to help us out. We have lost the simplicity of the disciple whose eyes are sharply focused on the love and the demand of God because there is no other source of security to cloud her vision.

Of course, there is no virtue in poverty for its own sake. And there are some fine examples of wealthy people who are generous with their money and their homes, and without whom the church's mission would be in a severe state of paralysis. But the numbing effects of prosperity are a snare to us all. Not for nothing did Jesus say that it's easier to thread a needle with a camel than for a rich man to enter the kingdom of God.

And what is true for individual Christians is true for churches also. They can come to rely more on the wealth of their traditions, the stability of their income and the efficiency of their systems than on the living God. Even their success in winning people to faith can become a means of congratulating themselves on being superior to other churches. Once, maybe, they used to say, 'Lord, we long for you to make yourself known to us and to our neighbours, and we depend on you because without you we can do nothing.' Now they say, 'How rich I am! I have everything I want.'

The Laodicean church was afflicted with a blindness which prevented them seeing that all this was happening to them. Their blindness must have taken other forms too. For example, they must surely have known about the sufferings experienced by some of the other churches of Asia. What they didn't know they could easily find out if they troubled to do so. For travellers were constantly passing their door. But they showed no sign of sympathizing with their fellow-Christians in other places. Perhaps they even took their own affluence as a sign of God's favour on them, and suspected that if other Christians suffered it was probably their own fault.

That kind of blindness is a common disease today. There are many churches who are pleased with their own performance but have little practical concern for the struggling inner-city church three miles away. There are many who give minimal priority to the church in other countries. They may even support a missionary working, say, in Brazil, but they have no sense of being bound in Christian fellowship with churches in Brazil and with Brazilian believers.

A church is naked when it fails to wear the character of Christ. What church can say that it constantly reflects in its life the character and concerns of Christ?

- Jesus' character is marked by self-giving. The church is sometimes marked by self-preservation.

- Jesus is always loving. The church is sometimes bickering over petty things.

● Jesus is concerned about the lost, the outcast, the people on the edge of society. The church usually prefers not to be disturbed by them.

● Jesus gets his hands dirty. The church likes to keep them clean.

● Jesus accepts suffering as the way to bring life to others. The church wants life, but prefers to avoid suffering.

● Jesus reflects the character of God. The church so often reflects simply the character of the society where it is placed.

The invitation of love

Despite its desperate complacency, the church is an object of Christ's love. 'Those whom I love I rebuke and discipline. So be earnest and repent' (verse 19). The very harshness of his criticism is a mark of the love which longs for the best and is satisfied with nothing less. So the exposure of the church's emptiness is followed by an invitation: 'I counsel you to buy from me gold refined in the fire, so that you can become rich; and white clothes to wear, so that you can cover your shameful nakedness; and salve to put on your eyes, so that you can see' (verse 18). In pointed contrast with the city's and the church's pride in what they have gained by their own achievements, the risen Christ invites them to 'buy from me' what no one else can supply.

The church is poor. Christ can make it truly rich with the kind of gold which he offers. But it is 'gold refined in the fire'. Gold becomes pure only by the refining process which burns out the dross. The Laodicean Christians cannot expect to find true riches without pain. Just as a parent knows that children can only learn some lessons 'the hard way', so Christ suggests that the rediscovery of his love will only come through the discipline of suffering. 'Those whom I love I rebuke and discipline' (verse 19).

The church is blind. But Christ can apply the ointment of his healing to enable it to see its own need and to renew its vision of his purpose.

The church is naked. But Christ can clothe it, not with black robes but with white, the clothing of the heavenly kingdom (see Rev. 3:4-5). In Revelation 6:11 Christian martyrs are given white robes. And in 19:6-8, when the 'wedding day of the Lamb' finally arrives, his bride the church is given 'fine linen, bright and clean', to wear. This fine linen, John explains, signifies the righteous deeds of God's people. Only Christ can make people fit to share in God's kingdom. Only he can transform proud, self-sufficient people into Christians whose righteous character reflects his own.

If Christ alone can transform a church's poverty, blindness and nakedness, there is in a sense nothing we can do to make things better. And the whole problem with a church like Laodicea is that it is blissfully unaware of its own tragic condition. On the surface it may look impressive, whilst underneath it has no deep roots into Christ. Yet it may have a few members who sense its shallowness and long for it to become more truly Christian. Perhaps they can help the church to ask some questions which will enable its members to think about their life and responsibilities as God's people.

From poverty to riches

● What would it mean for the church to discover 'gold refined in the fire'?

● If true riches don't come without pain, are we living in a way calculated to avoid persecution? Are we, for example, more concerned to be acceptable to society than to live by the uncomfortable demands of Christ?

● Are we prepared to share in suffering of other kinds – giving time and energy to those experiencing long-term illness, bereavement or loneliness, or those ignored and despised by society? Are we helping to bear the pressure felt by Christians who do face active persecution, by keeping in touch with some of them and praying imaginatively for them? Do we share in what Paul describes at the climax of a list of his sufferings, 'the pressure of my concern for all the churches' (2 Cor. 11:28)?

From blindness to vision

● Are we stumbling along, or plodding routinely along, content simply to survive but blind to the opportunities and challenges which God is putting before us? Does our church have a vision, a set of goals into which we believe God wants us to put our prayer and our energy? What kind of a church do we hope to be in five or ten years' time? Do we give practical expression to our vision for the future by taking our young people seriously?

● Are we genuinely open to the possibility that the living God might direct us to serve him in new and even risky ways? Does the church allow scope – in its worship and preaching, its prayer and policy-making meetings – for us to listen to God's call, to feel the tug of his Spirit?

From nakedness to being clothed with Christ's character

● Are we showing a quality of life which reminds people of Christ – his compassion, his lack of self-concern, his ability to let people know that they are valued, his singleminded commitment to God's will?

● Do we depend on Christ's power to clothe us with his character?

A knock at the door

There was one part of their history that the people of Laodicea would have preferred to forget. For several years during the first century BC their city, like others in Asia, was at the mercy of ruthless Roman governors who imposed crippling taxation and billeted their armies in people's homes. They were forced to pay a daily sum to the soldiers and to provide them with dinner. The self-sufficient independence of Laodicea which we have described above was no doubt partly a reaction to this kind of abuse.

The rebuilding of the city after the earthquake of AD 60 would include restoration of its gates, and we know from an inscription that the Syrian Gate was rebuilt in a particularly impressive style shortly before the writing of Revelation. Now at last, people might say to each other, we can decide who comes in and who is kept out.

Verse 20 must be read in this light. 'Here I am! I stand at the door and knock. If anyone hears my voice and opens the door, I will come in and eat with him, and he with me.' Christ will not force an entry. His coming is not a threat, but a precious promise to the individual who will invite him in. The dinner which they will eat together is not extorted at the point of a spear, but is the symbol of an enduring friendship.

It is striking that after so far addressing the whole Laodicean church together, Christ begins here to speak of 'anyone'. This implies that the invitation to open the door is addressed to each church member individually. Each one needs personally to put complacency aside and open himself to Christ's love. Each one has her name on an invitation to the dinner which will mark the beginning of a new relationship with Christ. Nevertheless, this message is not just about Christ's relationship to the individual Christian. It is the church, the whole group of Christians, which he wants to transform.

And the message keeps on coming. Will the church open wide its doors so that Christ may enter to fill it with his life? Or will it keep him out? An African discovered that he was not welcome in a 'white' church. In his anger and despair he was comforted by a vision of Christ, who said to him, 'Never mind, brother. I've tried to get into that church for years, and I haven't managed it yet!'

Christ not only binds himself in relationship to those who are open to his loving discipline, he shares his throne with them! (verse 21). Just as he promised in the letter to Thyatira that the victorious ones would share in his 'authority over the nations' (Rev. 2:26), so now he promises that they will share in the victory of his kingdom.

Listen to the Spirit!

So the letter, like all the others, reaches its urgent climax: 'Let anyone who has an ear listen to what the Spirit is saying to the churches' (verse 22). We may have ways of covering our ears; we may allow other sounds to drown his voice. But he does not give up on us. His love finds a way of confronting us once again with the challenge: will we let him raise us from our mediocrity into a new vitality? Will we let his concerns and priorities become ours? Are we ready to say, 'Whatever the cost to our earthly prosperity, we will open the door to his love'?

Questions for reflection and discussion

1. What particularly in this chapter has helped you or made you think?

2. 'You say, "I am rich; I have acquired wealth and do not need a thing." But you do not realize that you are wretched, pitiful, poor, blind and naked' (Rev. 3:17). How is it possible for a church to be so totally self-deceived? How can the danger be avoided?

3. Do you agree that wealthier churches have a special responsibility to support churches which are poorer because of where they are located or particular problems which they face? How can such support be offered without becoming a means by which the wealthier church controls the poorer one, rather than allowing it to develop in its own way?

4. 'What kind of a church do we hope to be in five or ten years' time?' (page 128). How important is it for a church to have a united vision of where it is going? What is your vision for your church five years from now?

*T*hen I saw a new heaven and a new earth, for the first heaven and the first earth had passed away, and there was no longer any sea. I saw the Holy City, the new Jerusalem, coming down out of heaven from God, prepared as a bride beautifully dressed for her husband. And I heard a loud voice from the throne saying, "Now the dwelling of God is with men, and he will live with them. They will be his people, and God himself will be with them and be their God. He will wipe every tear from their eyes. There will be no more death or mourning or crying or pain, for the old order of things has passed away."

He who was seated on the throne said, "I am making everything new!" Then he said, "Write this down, for these words are trustworthy and true."

He said to me: "It is done. I am the Alpha and the Omega, the Beginning and the End. To him who is thirsty I will give to drink without cost from the spring of the water of life. He who overcomes will inherit all this, and I will be his God and he will be my son. But the cowardly, the unbelieving, the vile, the murderers, the sexually immoral, those who practise magic arts, the idolaters and all liars — their place will be in the fiery lake of burning sulphur. This is the second death."

One of the seven angels who had the seven bowls full of the seven last plagues came and said to me, "Come, I will show you the bride, the wife of the Lamb." And he carried me away in the Spirit to a mountain great and high, and showed me the Holy City, Jerusalem, coming down out of heaven from God. It shone with the glory of God, and its *brilliance was like that of a very precious jewel, like a jasper, clear as crystal. The twelve gates were twelve pearls, each gate made of a single pearl. The great street of the city was of pure gold, like transparent glass.*

I did not see a temple in the city, because the Lord God Almighty and the Lamb are its temple. The city does not need the sun or the moon to shine on it, for the glory of God gives it light, and the Lamb is its lamp. The nations will walk by its light, and the kings of the earth will bring their splendour into it. On no day will its gates ever be shut, for there will be no night there. The glory and honour of the nations will be brought into it. Nothing impure will ever enter it, nor will anyone who does what is shameful or deceitful, but only those whose names are written in the Lamb's book of life.

Then the angel showed me the river of the water of life, as clear as crystal, flowing from the throne of God and of the Lamb down the middle of the great street of the city. On each side of the river stood the tree of life, bearing twelve crops of fruit, yielding its fruit every month. And the leaves of the tree are for the healing of the nations. No longer will there be any curse. The throne of God and of the Lamb will be in the city, and his servants will serve him. They will see his face, and his name will be on their foreheads. There will be no more night. They will not need the light of a lamp or the light of the sun, for the Lord God will give them light. And they will reign for ever and ever.

The angel said to me, "These words are trustworthy and true. The Lord, the God of the spirits of the prophets, sent an angel to show his servants the things that must soon take place."

"Behold, I am coming soon! My reward is with me, and I will give to everyone according to what he has done. I am the Alpha and the Omega, the First and the Last, the Beginning and the End.

"Blessed are those who wash their robes, that they may have the right to the tree of life and may go through the gates into the city. Outside are the dogs, those who practise magic arts, the sexually immoral, the murderers, the idolaters and everyone who loves and practises falsehood.

"I, Jesus, have sent my angel to give you this testimony for the churches. I am the Root and the Offspring of David, and the bright Morning Star."

The Spirit and the bride say, "Come!" And let him who hears say, "Come!" Whoever is thirsty, let him come; and whoever wishes, let him take the free gift of the water of life.

I warn everyone who hears the words of the prophecy of this book: If anyone adds anything to them, God will add to him the plagues described in this book. And if anyone takes words away from this book of prophecy, God will take away from him his share in the tree of life and in the holy city, which are described in this book.

He who testifies to these things says, "Yes, I am coming soon."

Amen. Come, Lord Jesus.

The grace of the Lord Jesus be with God's people. Amen.

Revelation 21:1-11, 21-27; 22:1-7, 12-21

CHAPTER 9

The Lord who comes

(Revelation 21–22)

Our tour is completed. We have travelled with John's messenger to each of the seven churches. We have listened with those churches to the words of the risen Lord to his people. We have tried to ask what it means for us to 'listen to what the Spirit is saying to the churches'. In the course of studying what Christ thinks of the seven churches, we have had to reckon with what he thinks of us. We now draw together some key themes from the letters.

First, Christ knows intimately our church and the pressures and opportunities it faces. If he knew so well the churches and cities of Asia, he knows us too. Whether we are facing a huge bill for re-roofing our building, or overwhelmed by the challenge presented by the homeless in our streets, or rejoicing at the opportunities we have to share the good news with young people, he knows and understands. He is not content with our narrow horizons or deceived by our compromises. He is not defeated by our weakness. He delights in our faithfulness.

Secondly, the church is created and sustained by God's grace. It is not simply a human organization, but a people called into being by God's love. Christ blesses it with his presence. To two contrasting churches he speaks specifically of his love for them. By calling the Philadelphian Christians 'the people on whom I have set my love' (Rev. 3:9, my translation), he assures them of his care as they face hostile surroundings. By speaking of his love for the church at Laodicea (Rev. 3:19), he reminds them that even the most hopeless church remains within reach of his renewing power. Whatever the condition of a church, Christ holds it in his love.

Thirdly, if Christ offers unlimited love, he also makes great demands of the church. Having loved us and freed us from our sins, he calls us to service (Rev. 1:5-6). He makes his demand not as a ruthless taskmaster, but because his goal is to make us a people who reflect God's character and who share effectively in God's mission to the world. But he never makes demands without promising supernatural resources to meet them. Every letter begins with a reminder of Christ's power and ends with promises of what he will do for his people.

The fact that two churches receive praise rather than criticism implies that it is possible in the strength of Christ to remain faithful under pressure. So the other churches have no reason to excuse themselves by saying, 'Well, this was all we could manage in the circumstances.'

Fourthly, Christ speaks to each church as a community of brothers and sisters. In the individualistic atmosphere of the modern world we are inclined to read the warnings and promises of Scripture as messages to individuals. And we think of our Christian commitment as 'my faith', 'my relationship with God'. That is important, but it is only half the story. In belonging to Christ we belong with each other.

It is true that the closing words of each letter focus on the response of individuals within the churches – 'let anyone who has an ear...'; 'those who are victorious...' Each message calls for a personal response, a personal contribution to the church's renewal. But the main thrust of each letter is a message to the church as a community of Christians whose lives interlock with each other. It is especially as a community that we bear witness to the transforming power of Christ. In a competitive society driven by material values, it is as a community that we demonstrate the possibility of living by distinctive Christian principles.

For some Christians who struggle with the institutional life of the church this stress on a collective discipleship does not come easily. But how would the persecuted churches of both the first and the twenty-first centuries react to the kind of Christian who stands aloof from the ordinary life of a local church? Perhaps they would want gently to insist that such individualism is a luxury we cannot afford if we are to resist the forces which oppose us.

Fifthly, churches face a great variety of pressures. At Ephesus, it seems that the very success of the Christian mission has provoked a revival of pagan religion and a consequent battle over moral standards. Other churches are surrounded by hostile Jews, who have no desire that Christians should benefit from whatever protection they themselves have under the law. Some have to decide whether taking part in emperor-worship is a betrayal of Christ or simply a harmless social convention.

Others are wrestling with the dilemma of how flexible Christian freedom can be: has Christ set us free to do anything we like, or are there certain boundaries to Christian behaviour? In some churches there are serious divisions between rival groups. The church at Laodicea, on the other hand, is united in its deadly complacency. In all this variety we see, as in a mirror, aspects of the life and surroundings of today's churches.

If a local church is to be healthy and effective, its leaders must identify the pressures it faces and teach people to understand and respond to them. If an army doesn't know its enemy it will fail at the first hint of battle. Yet so much preaching and teaching in the church today lacks a cutting edge because it is bland and general.

We are often afraid to tackle with any thoroughness the forces which shape people's lives and make it hard for Christians to be confident and wholehearted in their faith. Or we console ourselves with the thought that, if we tried to teach people more thoroughly and systematically, 'they couldn't take it'. Often, though not always, such a comment betrays more about our superficial and unstrategic approach as leaders than about church members' commitment to the way of Christ.

Sixthly, different churches may have very different states of health. Some, like Smyrna and Philadelphia, may deserve nothing but praise from Christ. Others, like Sardis and Laodicea, have almost ceased to be churches in any sense that Christ would recognize. And it is, after all, his view which counts. Christians down the years have fondly assumed that churches are automatically on the side of God, and he is on their side. The letters of Revelation show this to be a dangerous delusion. The grace of God cannot be taken for granted.

Churches would be healthier if they had a truer picture of what they were meant to be. For many the church is a club , which they have joined because they like its activities. They have a club committee which thinks up interesting things to do. They have special club get-togethers on Sunday mornings, with a team talk from the chief coach. They like it this way, and are not too concerned about persuading other people to join, so long as the club remains solvent. Other people think of the church as a haven, a place of peace and stability in the middle of an uncomfortable world. They want it to stay as it has always been, the one secure harbour in a sea of change.

But if we ask how John views the church, two pictures predominate. The church is a *bride*, whose single desire is to prepare herself for marriage to her Lord. Nothing matters to her more than that she should please him and be in tune with his concerns (Rev. 19:7-8).

And the church is an *army*. John is using military language when, in each of the seven letters, he refers to 'him who overcomes', or 'those who are victorious'. Christians are engaged in a battle, which they fight with the weapons of love and faith, service and suffering. And belonging to an army requires discipline, single-mindedness and total obedience to the commanding officer.

Seventhly, God has an ultimate goal for the church. John shows this by his careful linking of the promises to 'those who are victorious' with the vision of the new heaven and new earth in Revelation 21-22. Whatever the state of the churches now, whatever the intensity of the battle between good and evil, whatever the circumstances through which God's people will be forced to pass – Christ's triumph will in the end mean that those who remain faithful to him will experience in full all that God longs to give them. One day Christ will come finally to complete the work of salvation which he began in Bethlehem, in Nazareth and in Jerusalem. On that day his people will at last see beyond their weakness, their suffering and all the ambiguities of the present life, to the perfect goal which he has in store for them.

Let us see, then, how the promises of chapters 2-3 are taken up.

A new heaven and a new earth

The day will come when the old order dominated by Rome, and later by other political powers, is replaced by 'the Holy City, new Jerusalem, coming down out of heaven from God' (21:2). So the promise to Philadelphia, of a new Jerusalem where they will not be subject to Jewish abuse (Rev. 3:12), will be fulfilled. Then God will have his dwelling with mankind (21:3). Though now his presence is mysterious, and sometimes seems remote, then faith will give way to sight.

Then God will supply his people with 'the water of life' (21:6), which will flow from his throne down the street of the City (22:2). What the church at Laodicea could not supply for itself and was refusing to receive from Christ will be freely available to all who admit their thirst (21:6; 22:17).

The sense of space and safety in the new Jerusalem is in complete contrast with the constant danger and uncer- tainty to which John's contemporaries are exposed. But, in case their experience should make them think that earthly rulers are always destined to suppress the truth and oppress God's people, John offers a vision of the nations coming to the City in worship. 'The nations will walk by its light, and the kings of the earth will bring their splendour into it... The glory and honour of the nations will be brought into it' (21:24, 26). Whenever we are tempted to dismiss the varieties of human culture and to think of the whole world - apart from ourselves or our group - as hopelessly embroiled in evil, we need to remember that God has other plans.

On either bank of the river of the water of life stands the 'tree of life', providing the promised nourishment for the City's people (22:2, 14; 2:7). That God's servants belong securely in his presence is shown by the writing of his name on their foreheads (22:4; compare 3:12).

Jesus himself, whose final coming will herald the fulfil- ment of all these expectations, is described in terms which recall the seven letters. He is 'the Root and Offspring of David, and the bright Morning Star' (22:16). The stress on the Messiah's descent from David reassures John's readers – particularly those at Smyrna and Philadelphia – that as followers of Jesus they truly belong to God's people. In call- ing himself the Morning Star Christ repeats the phrase which affirmed to the Thyatiran church both his messianic credentials and his superiority over the emperor (Rev. 2:28).

Domitian may think he rules the world, but his post is merely temporary.

'I am coming soon'

The refrain comes three times in the final chapter: 'I am coming soon' (22:7, 12, 20). The most important thing about the church's Lord is that he is on his way to fulfil the promises he has made. The whole book of Revelation strains towards that final, glorious climax of all God's action in history. At his final coming Christ will hold all people to account for their lives (22:12), and will bring to those who trust in God all the blessings described in Revelation 21-22.

But what does 'soon' mean? If the final coming of Christ is 'soon' for us, how could it also be 'soon' for John's first readers nineteen hundred years ago? In keeping with the poetic and pictorial style of Revelation, it is not the 'soon' of calendar time: 'Inflation will soon reach double figures. In fact, next month's retail price index is expected to show a sharp increase.' It is the 'soon' of a certain promise, as when a child is told, 'Mummy is coming soon' – meaning that, though the child cannot grasp what this may imply in terms of hours and minutes, Mummy will without question come because she has promised to come and she will not let her child down.

So Christ's final coming may happen at any time. The important thing is not that it will necessarily take place in the near future, but that it is intended by a God who keeps his promises. And the Christ who will come in the end is the same Christ who is constantly coming, in blessing and judgment, to his people. So the churches are called not to speculate about the timing of the final coming, but to take seriously the comings of Christ in their present experience.

How will the Christians of Ephesus respond to his warning, 'If you do not repent, I will come to you and remove your lampstand from its place' (Rev. 2:5)?

How will the adherents of false teaching at Pergamum react to his message, 'So repent! If you do not, I will come to you quickly and make war on them with the sword that comes out of my mouth' (Rev. 2:16)?

Will the church at Sardis listen to him when he says, 'If you do not wake up, I will come upon you like a thief' (Rev. 2:3)?

Will the Christians at Philadelphia take courage from his promise, 'I am coming soon; hold fast to what you have, and let no one rob you of your crown' (Rev. 3:11)?

Will Laodicea stir from its slumbers in response to his invitation, 'If anyone hears my voice and opens the door, I will come in and he and I will eat together' (Rev. 3:20)?

The same questions come to us. Sometimes Christ confronts us with insistent urgency, perhaps through a preacher or through a situation that cries out for a reaction. At other times he creeps up on us like a lover surprising his beloved, warming our hearts with his presence. But however he comes, the question is the same: what will we do with the invitation and the demand which he holds out to us? Will we strain our ears to hear and to respond to what he is saying to us and to our church today?

A child wrote: 'I don't think Jesus will come back again. He's gone off people.'

The message of Revelation is that Jesus has not gone off people, but that he stays with us through good times and bad. He stands by his promise, 'I am coming soon'. And he looks for a church which, by its life in the world as well as in its worship, is responding, 'Amen. Come, Lord Jesus' (22:20).

Questions for reflection and discussion

1. What particularly in this chapter has helped you or made you think?

2. 'If an army doesn't know its enemy it will fail at the first hint of battle' (page 138). What do you think are the main enemies which the church faces, and how can we 'know' them so that we do not 'fail when the battle comes'?

3. Think about the pictures of the world to come which God promises to his people in these chapters. Which pictures or promises do you find particularly reassuring? Do you think Christians give enough thought to God's 'ultimate goal for the church'?

4. In what ways has your reading of this book affected your view of your church, your hopes and fears for its future?

5. In what ways has your reading of this book affected your understanding of Christ and your appreciation of his role as Saviour and Lord of the church?